Tiffany is a founding partner of RoundTable Global, an international award-winning leadership development organisation, where she is focusing full time on her desire to create empowerment and balance in the world. She is passionate about creating corporations and communities that are creative and compassionate as well as commercial and believes that by empowering leaders to authentically tap into both their masculine and feminine energies, we can redefine social and business norms, unlock potential and ultimately create fearless cultures where effortless change will happen in the world around us. She is also an inspirational speaker leading women's empowerment workshops, leadership summits and innovation think tanks towards social change.

GW00642979

In loving memory of my father, John Kelly, who tragically passed while I was writing this book.

To my beautiful, big hearted dad...
I will not remember you as the man you became,
I will remember you always as one of my best friends,
Your long rejuvenating hugs and throw-your-head-back laugh,
The way you advised me and guided my path,
We had so many adventures, could share feelings with a glance,
We were always the last ones standing, no one else stood a chance,
You taught me your dance moves and how to really love,
Two peas in a pod, your hand fit mine like a glove,
You made me feel safe and taught me to be graceful,
For the wisdom you shared I will always be grateful,
You were the life and soul of gatherings with friends,
We are your legacy, your beginning and end,
I miss you immensely, so intensely, my heart feels lost,
You were a special kind of divine more empathic than most,
Everyone who knew you has a story of your kindness,
Your huge hearted unconditional love helped all of us,
You were charming and talented, gorgeous and funny,
I miss your beautiful smile, the way you called me honey,
I will never ever forget to be the person you were proud of,
Every morning I will think of you and send you some love,
Goodbye my lovely dad, be at peace now you rest,
My memories of you will always be the best,
Thank you for my sisters, in them I see you,
In us your spirit lives on, this I know will always be true,
So, it is time for us now to celebrate your life,
To share memories together and cherish your wife,
Know that you were loved by everyone here,
We will never forget you; we will always hold you dear.

Tiffany Kelly

SHINE

Effortless Abundance

AUSTIN MACAULEY PUBLISHERS™

LONDON • CAMBRIDGE • NEW YORK • SHARJAH

ISBN 9781528991216 (Paperback)
ISBN 9781528991223 (ePub e-book)

www.austinmacauley.com

First Published (2020)
Austin Macauley Publishers Ltd
25 Canada Square
Canary Wharf
London
E14 5LQ

There are so many people that I would like to express deep gratitude to for inspiring, empowering and enabling me to imagine and write this book. To some extent, the process itself has felt effortless with the words almost writing themselves. I put this down to how certain I am of our offering and how keen I am to share the learnings with you all. So, first of all I would like to thank every single person who purchases this book and starts the journey. The effortlessness and speed of getting the philosophies out there has been your co-creation.

I want to primarily thank my co-founder and teacher Denis Murphy, without whom RoundTable Global and these philosophies would not exist. Thank you from the bottom of my heart for everything you have shared with and shown to me.

To Charlotte Dillon, who taught me so much about creativity and imagination and to my sister, Tanith, who stepped up into the helm beside me when her energy and enthusiasm was needed so much – thank you.

To my closest friends, who have held and supported me through my trying times as I was writing, you will never know just how much I appreciate your love and laughter. And to Nick, who created a beautiful space for me to heal and write, I am immensely grateful.

To the RoundTable Global core leadership team, Ulpa, Zoe, Jacqui, Becky, Raquel, Erin, Tom and our amazing and inspiring Global Change Ambassadors – thank you for contributing to *Shine* in your own beautiful ways.

To my mentors, Rob Chalis and David Williams, thank you for your encouragement, wisdom and support. I would not be where I am today without you.

Lastly and most importantly, to my mum and Les, you taught me so much about myself, that I could do and be anything and for that I will always be grateful.

To everyone else in my life, who has been with me on the journey and been inspired by *Shine* – thank you. It is with so much love and gratitude, that I finish writing this book.

Table of Contents

'After going through the Shine journey, I have experienced an incredible re-connection with my Self. After years of seeking, I see so clearly my power and potential, and the opportunities that are available to me in any given moment. Once the Shine teachings settle, the affect is profound. The Shine gift is a transformational, limitless belief system that one can never un-know.'
– Claire Bates

'A tenacious, discerning, delivery of thought provoking, expansive, life changing philosophies, explained with great intention, articulation and care in such a way the experience was just wonderful, especially with the after care and future Learning possibilities.
I received a deep sense of nurturing, and know that subtle differences will appear in my personal eco system which will reflect on every aspect of my future journey as a leader and on a personal level.'
– Gillian Kirkham

'SHINE is an amazing journey of exploration and discovery. I didn't know what to expect and I was just swept off my feet! I've learnt so much about myself. I feel confident about the steps I will take next to empower myself and empower others.
I want to recommend this programme to everyone I know to share the privilege of these insights. It's been so different from every personal development journey I've been on before; it dives deep in your emotions and really enables you to connect with your real self.'
– Catherine Serusclat

'Thanks again, Tiffany, for creating Shine. It has really been a brilliant journey and a great developmental moment for me – definitely one of the best leadership courses I have been through since I started at Danone 18 years ago. My colleagues clearly noticed a change in my mindset (more confident: "Stars in the eyes" etc.). Something has happened in my life and you're responsible for that change.'

– Julie Bourget

Introduction

I am shining right now. I can say that without ego or arrogance because I have finally stepped courageously into my authentic self. For the first time in my life I am truly bringing everything that I am to everything that I do. I am fearless and limitless in a way that I have never been before and the energy I am broadcasting is effortlessly attracting beautiful like-minded individuals to teach, learn, share and create with me.

This year I will be 42 years old and I am excited about every step towards that milestone knowing that I am not attached to what being 42 means. That the label of age and the expectations that come with it no longer permeate my thoughts and feelings with fear.

I have 41 years of experience on this planet. A mere drop in the ocean of the Earths existence and yet I have already lived and already left a mark. I have loved, laughed, lost and left a legacy, the power of which I am only just fully understanding.

In the last ten years I have had the privilege to work with people all over the world delivering talks, projects and programmes of personal leadership and empowerment and I have discovered that the thing that most resonates and creates mindset and behaviour change is our ability to connect and share. Our ability to create a space where we can learn from each other without judgement, where we can see the mirror that is being held up to us in the experiences we create and take full responsibility for the learning.

It is from this place that comes the realisation of how awe inspiring and perfect the gift of life on this planet can be. Living authentically without fear and judgement has enabled me to see the lessons and synchronicities I have created to take me on this great journey. To look back now and understand that what I experienced as bullying in my teenage years taught me the skills, I am using today means that I am able to change my past. I am able to understand that with the benefit of time and a change of perception, every single thing that has happened in my life has served me in some way. Every single thing.

It is mind blowing to think in this way. Mind blowing and unbelievably liberating and I will be forever grateful to Denis Murphy, who patiently taught me these things.

I have always known that I had a story inside me, a slow unfolding of thoughts and ideas and I am filled with excitement as it is finally spilling out of me.

Shine is a story and a way of life; it is my gift to you. An offer of a different way of living that will help you to become empowered and rejuvenated. It is based on my personal experiences and a global leadership programme that I designed with my partners at RoundTable Global.

It will take you through the process of better understanding yourself and the power of your beliefs. It will help you to more clearly see the strengths and passions that make you who you are and how to fully leverage them. My intention is that it inspires you to be fearless about your unique individuality, to become more authentic and to create leadership action in your life that is empowering for you and for everyone else around you.

I ask you to read this book slowly and patiently and to be gentle with yourself as you practice the ideas and philosophies I have offered. It is a book that can be shared with loved ones of all ages, an opportunity for you to really reconnect with yourself and the people in your eco-system.

There is a deliberate journey of awareness and development as you read through the chapters with ideas and examples building on each other and my personal story unfolding as you read. This being said, the journey is yours and how ever the pages open themselves to you will be the perfect way for you to read it.

I believe in the power of synchronicity meaning that there is no such thing as a coincidence and that you are reading this book now because it is the right time for you.

Having taken so many people through this journey in person over the past four years I am excited for you. Every person who has been through Shine has transformed in some way and I believe that by putting this process down on paper my partners and I will be able to create a global butterfly effect of change towards enjoyment, authenticity and ultimately love.

Marianne Williamson said, *'Our deepest fear is not that we are inadequate. Our deepest fear is that we are powerful beyond measure. It is our light, not our darkness that most frightens us. We ask ourselves, who am I to be brilliant, gorgeous, talented, and fabulous? Actually, who are you not to be? ...You're playing small does not serve the world. There is nothing enlightened about shrinking so that other people will not feel insecure around you. We are all meant to shine, as children do. We were born to make manifest the glory that is within us. It is not just in some of us; it is in everyone and as we let our own light shine, we unconsciously give others permission to do the same. As we are liberated from our own fear, our presence automatically liberates others.'*

Check In

How often do we check in with ourselves? How often do we stop for a moment, close our eyes and allow our bodies to tell us what we need to know about how we are feeling? Up until two years I never gave this gift to myself. I was never truly present in the moment, my mind racing towards what was next, my to do list and all of the achievements I needed to make before growing too old to make them.

Now, at the beginning of every programme and event we run, we ensure that everyone in the room checks in. We are all busy people with a tremendous amount of distractions and stimulations in our lives and it can at first feel uncomfortable to be completely still with our thoughts and to listen to our bodies.

We think that it is only our senses that provide us with information but actually every single cell in our bodies is constantly communicating with our conscious and subconscious mind. We don't fully appreciate this because any time we feel something we block the sensation with pharmaceutical drugs or learn to adapt through fitness, yoga, massage and other relievers of tension.

Our bodies are talking to us and there is so much that can be learned from teaching ourselves to listen. In fact, what I have found is that when we create an opportunity to check in and to authentically share whatever comes into our minds in a non-judgemental environment, the most beautiful realisations and connections are made.

Sharing something of yourself during a check in gives you the permission to be honest about how you are feeling and it gives those around your permission to do the same. I have been surprised and delighted by the overwhelming emotions and disclosures that come tumbling out in the first 10 minutes of a programme. Even individuals who have worked with each other for 20 years always find out something new, they see the unique human being behind the persona created for work.

Strangers checking in together immediately build a circle of empathy and support and this creates relationships and experiences that they are keen to continue.

I don't fully understand yet why we have created a society where we have to put on a brave face and be strong all of the time, why the feminine leadership qualities are seen as weaknesses when what I have experienced is the complete opposite. It takes courage to be honest, to allow the facade to dissolve and to bring the real you into the room. Most people spend so much time living as the person they think everyone wants them to be that this bringing of self into the moment can be an extremely vulnerable, powerful and transformational experience.

The check in that created this feeling in me was when I delivered my first female empowerment programme in a temple in Tokyo in 2014. Standing in my socks in a circle of 12 women from one of the most repressed countries in the world who were honestly sharing how tired, frustrated and sad they were made me realise that I needed to change my entire life. It struck me hard like a blow to the solar plexus as I listened and realised how much of my life was fake positive and coping.

In that moment I felt truly authentic and able to share my whole self with the group, in fact they needed it from me so that they could follow. I found myself sharing my inner most fears and the knowledge of the need for change that my subconscious had been protecting me from began seeping into my conscious mind for the first time.

I didn't love my job or my work place. I was successful, well paid, had autonomy and opportunity but I was existing in a fear driven culture that had become a self-fulfilling prophecy of doubt about our ability to effortlessly succeed. I was working in a male dominated industry with masculine leadership and I was constantly striving to prove myself as a woman. I was overcompensating for my gender by working harder and longer. Not taking holidays and being 'so busy' were badges of honour worn and shared whenever our teams converged.

I know now that I created all of this, that I needed to build that drive to succeed to do the things that I have done but I also know now that life does not have to be hard and that we can work less and achieve more. That we can create a balance in our lives where work and life doesn't exist, it is all life and the experiences we create can be enriching, lucrative and fulfil our innate desire for adventure and to give back but I will come on to that later.

My other realisation that day was to do with my marriage and that I needed to leave the person I had created a whole life with so that we could both become truly happy. Our compromises and attempts to be joyful together were hard work and the energy and will power it took was making us both ill. Someone told me once that marriages are hard and need to be worked at and I simply do not believe that to be true. If our bodies and environments are shouting at us and showing us how much tension and stress, we are under the greatest gift we can give to ourselves and to the other person is to leave.

To reiterate, I am offering my experiences and beliefs for you to do with what you wish. Everything we create in our lives it to learn from and the timescale for that learning is different for everyone.

That check in, that moment of listening and authenticity changed my entire life and I will never be the same again.

As I looked at the closed eyed faces of the women in the room and took them through the process of feeling and listening to their bodies, I felt my own shoulders relax and drop when I hadn't even realised they were tense and I realised how unbelievably tired my body was.

As they took their deep breaths and committed to what they would share the words that had been deep inside me rushed to my lips and I set the scene by admitting that everything in my life needed to change.

Social conditioning to be happy and positive and the pressure to achieve is heavy. It weighs on every ounce of our beings like a lead weight around our necks. Tension creeps from the neck to shoulders, lower back and finally our legs over a period of time and before we realise it, before we choose to listen there is something serious that we cannot ignore anymore. At this time, I was suffering from shingles at least once a month and had been for over two years. My body was screaming at me to make a change and finally I did.

I no longer believe in labelling the messages that my body gives to me but for you to understand the debilitating pain I had created and how relevant it was I need to share with you the medical diagnosis. For those that don't know, shingles attacks the nervous system and outbreaks appear as angry painful rashes that burn. The life I was living was full of anxiety and I didn't know how to be still in it any longer. The perfect manifestation of shingles on my lower torso meant that I couldn't sit down and constantly needed to move.

My body was talking to me and it definitely wasn't subtle.

The final catalyst for change was when I developed a consistent twitch in my right thumb, the one you use when you are indicating something is OK. For six months, it tried to get my attention and visibly show me how I was feeling but I had taken the doctor's recommendation for mild antidepressants to suppress the nervous system rather than listening.

The moment I left my old life, my thumb relaxed and the shingles disappeared. I haven't been to see a doctor since.

Now every day, I try to find time to check in with myself, to listen to my body and the chatter in my mind to see what I can learn from it. Nothing is random or irrelevant, it all means something and I am still on the journey of learning how to interpret this information and when it doesn't matter if you do or do not. The most important realisation for me is that we are listening and learning.

Most people I know believe that they are good listeners, but the reality is that the majority are simply hearing. The ability to really listen is a unique skill that will change the way you live your life. Because we are inherently an inwardly focused species, we are constantly making everything relevant to us. This means that when other people are speaking, we are thinking of what we want to say or how what is being said impacts or resonates with us. Rather than listening with 100% of our attention we are then waiting for the person to finish so that we can speak. We do this with children all of the time.

We feel the lack of attention and impatience for our turn energetically in each other and it means that depending on the confidence and perception of the person speaking, the stream of consciousness is not always able to flow. Also, most people believe that listening is something we do only with our ears and to external sources of sound but there are many variations of listening. It is just as important to listen with 100% attention to ourselves and the words/language that we are using as it is to listen to others. Developing this skill set provides a fascinating insight into the subconscious mind.

Our subconscious is full of what we don't know we know and is constantly trying to teach us about our limiting beliefs, patterns and behaviours so that we can clear from our stuff and life can be more effortless. When you learn to really listen to what you are saying, especially when you are speaking without thinking, you will find out how you really feel about things and why you are creating the world and reality you are.

We are often not even aware of the language we are using, what it means and the impact it has on our beliefs and ability to create.

We can also listen physically (is my body speaking to me and if so, what does it mean?), energetically (what am I feeling about this place, experience, person?) and by becoming more aware of our environment and asking questions about what it is teaching us.

Before I take you through the process of checking in, of fully being here and present with me and your experience of the words that follow I want to share with you how check ins can feature in every area of your life. They are extremely useful to empower teams when you are in a position of leadership, they disarm, defuse and demonstrate that we are all actually human, fallible and beautifully vulnerable.

They are magical when experienced with family, especially with partners and children. It used to be that family dinners around the table provided a time and place to share and support but in our fast, throw away and technology driven life styles these moments are now few and far between. Putting away your devices, having a moment of silence and stillness and then sharing brings to the surface things that are often buried deep.

Check ins are also a marker, a beginning of something and I love the idea that we have the ability to start our relationship with ourselves and the people we love, again as new, every single day. As if we are seeing and meeting them for the first time.

Action: The Check In

Stand up with your hands held loosely by your sides. Close your eyes. Find your balance. Inhale and exhale. Find a rhythm with your breath and really feel how the oxygen filling your lungs effects your body. Take your focus to your feet. Wiggle your toes if you need to. Imagine that you are a tree with roots stretching down deep into the earth. Inhale and exhale. Take your focus to your calves, up through your knees to your thighs. What do you feel? Is there any tension? What is your body telling you? Inhale and exhale. Take your attention to your hips and up through your stomach and into your chest. Are you breathing freely? We often hold stress in our stomach and chest. What do you notice? Inhale and exhale. Now move your focus to your shoulders and neck, are your shoulders loose, low and relaxed back? If not, how do they feel? How does your head feel on your neck? Inhale and exhale. Take your attention down through your arms to your hands and wiggle your fingers if you need to. Does your body feel like it needs to move at all? To adjust in some way. If it does allow that to happen. Focus on your arms again and up through your shoulders to your face. Is there any tension there? How does it feel? Two deep long breaths. Be still and listen. Now really listen.

Now ask yourself, how am I feeling today? What am I thinking? How would I like to check in? Then stand back and listen, see what comes without purposefully creating words in your head. Share with yourself or if you are with others share out loud. Be generous with your sharing and also your listening. Be honest, authentic and in the moment.

It may be useful for you to record yourself or someone else slowly reading out loud this process until you find your own way and rhythm for checking in. I personally enjoy hearing my partner speak the words so that I can follow the instructions and really connect without worrying about the process.

Homework:

In the next chapter we are going to explore perceptions of self and the impact that this has on our lives. To prepare yourself for this I recommend spending time with different people in your eco system and asking them how they perceive you. Listen and take notes. Do not be defensive but ask questions to clarify if you need to. This information is going to be invaluable. Read chapter 19 – Solo Reflection, you may find this process useful to do after every chapter.

After every chapter, I encourage you to notice what is different, not what is the same. Notice if your choices, interactions, desires, emotions and physical sensations are different. The more you notice differences, the more you open yourself to further effortless change.

Distorted Sense of Self

Do we ever really see ourselves? Can we look at ourselves in the mirror, listen to ourselves speak or make choices and decisions without criticising, looking for the negative and constantly highlighting the things about ourselves that we don't like? As children we learn this behaviour. Ask a young child what they don't like about themselves and you will see that mostly they find it easier to tell you what they love about themselves. It is only as they get older and learn from us, like sponges, that they start to doubt themselves and look for the flaws and faults that they either believe they have or create subconsciously to fit in.

Epigenetics teaches us that of course we are born with specific genes that create predispositions to certain things but that we have the power to switch these genes off or on based on our beliefs, which are ultimately created by our environment, culture and heritage. If we believe that all the women in our family have big hips, we actually have the ability to create them. The belief becomes a self-fulfilling prophecy, but more on that later.

At the beginning of the Shine programme we take all the participants one by one into a room and get them to record a one to three-minute video telling us about themselves. It is such a powerful, emotional process for them and absolutely no one that I have come across likes it. Initially we asked participants to film the videos pre-programme but it created so much stress and anxiety that we decided a surprise approach would work better.

Every person we have taken through this process finds it incredibly hard. The thought of being immortalised on camera without preparation, with no time to check makeup and hair is extremely uncomfortable and demonstrative of the online culture we have created where we only post what we want people to see and how we want them to perceive us. Filters, the ability to airbrush and even Photoshop, are all easily usable apps now and we have complete control over our online avatars.

It is not only the aesthetics of being caught on camera that causes stress it is the ambiguity of not knowing how the content will be used, not being able to plan what to say and practice how to say it. This is why I like this project so much. We see the real person, caught in a moment of vulnerability, showing their true selves to the camera. Or not as the case may be. What I mean by this is that some of our participants are so practiced at being who they think people want them to be that the mask easily slips on and they perform well. The exciting thing is that even with these people, you get a glimpse of what is going on underneath.

Later in the programme we sit in a circle and each person takes a turn to watch their video in front of the group, share what they see about who they are and how they come across and then sit back and listen as the rest of us share what we see. It is always very different.

The participant always talks first about the things they see that they don't like. Some can't even watch the video and some become very emotional as they 'hate seeing themselves'. I find this fascinating and extremely sad, especially knowing that I was in that place of self-doubt and distorted perception not so long ago. The word hate is powerful, it demonstrates to me that the person has deep rooted beliefs that are affecting their perception of both themselves and the world.

If you hate seeing yourself or hearing yourself, imagine the pressure and stress that this is creating in your body and your environment every single day. You will be constantly worrying about how you're coming across, how people are perceiving you and whether you are good enough.

A wonderful thing happens when the rest of us share what we see on the videos. Virtually everyone goes first to the thing that they enjoyed, admired or loved about the clip. They compare it immediately to what they have created and find something that they wish they had said or done. A sharing of something personal is admired as courageous and a genuine laugh or smile is seen as authentic, warm and approachable. The moments of vulnerability are appealing to the observers and they want to find out more about the person. The compliments are always generous and any constructive feedback is given in a gentle way. The participant whose video it is, can't help but smile and relax as they hear the rest of the group speak. They are always surprised by how differently the world sees them to how they see themselves.

Now part of this 'perception' of others is based on a comparison of how we see ourselves, how 'badly' we think we have done with our own videos but it doesn't matter. It is indicative of what happens in the world. In general, we look for things that we like in others, we want them to succeed and to do well. It is only our fears and self-limiting beliefs that create experiences where we look for faults in other people and mostly so that we can say we are right about them or so that we feel better about ourselves.

I believe that the human being is predisposed to love and kindness but that we have created a culture and society that is very masculine and encourages unhealthy competition. This means that we are constantly comparing ourselves to everyone else rather than enjoying our unique individuality.

For those that manage to slip into a 'work persona' when the camera is turned on, we can always see a bit of the real person at the beginning or end of the clip. You can see exactly when the mask goes on and when it comes off again and the feedback from the rest of the group is reflective of this. They might say for example 'you came across extremely professionally, it was like you had rehearsed what to say. I wish I could be more like that. I really loved it at the end though when you spoke about your children and it made you blush and laugh.' We don't need to be behaviour analysts to be able to see and feel authenticity, we admire the polished persona because the world teaches us that this creates success but we love the real person even more because ultimately we are human and I believe that all human beings have the potential to exist within a balance of both masculine and feminine energy.

Showing vulnerability is a feminine strength and we long for it in our very masculine lives. We long to connect and share and stop striving towards perfection. What does being perfect mean anyway? Who has defined it? We are constantly bombarded with messages from the media about how we should be, in one culture we are too white and need to darken to show that we are successful and healthy, in another culture we are too dark and need to bleach our skin and lighten our bodies to show that we are successful and healthy. The concept of being perfect is a tool of propaganda used to generate money for the health and beauty industries. It is also used as a way to keep us striving towards that ever-elusive perfection. Aesthetically and culturally speaking.

We long for vulnerability so much that is has actually become something that we can use to make people like us more. When I was at university in London, studying law, with a healthy mind and body, I found that people didn't always like me. They definitely wanted to be around me but behind closed doors they would talk about me as if I was arrogant and 'loved myself'. I know now that I was creating this situation because I was still in a victim mindset which I will talk more about later on but the important thing to mention now is that because of this 'bullying' I subconsciously created a medical illness. I started fainting all the time. My blood pressure would drop really low, my heart would speed up to compensate and ultimately, I would pass out. The timing was always when I was going through a 'tough time' and the vulnerability caused everyone to like me more.

One day as I was cycling to university I fainted in the middle of the road and it was at this point that I started to have tests done in the hospital. I found myself going through the same process as elderly people as they tried to work out what was wrong with me. Part of this process was wearing a heart tape for 24 hours with electrodes and pads attached across my chest as I went about my daily routine.

Everyone knew about it and I will never forget the moment when I was working my part time shift behind a bar in Liverpool Street Station and it hit home to me the reality of what I had created. I was singing as I cleaned the glasses and although I don't have an amazing voice I can carry a tune, when a colleague who suffered from polycystic ovaries amongst other things, came over to me and said, 'If you didn't have a problem with your heart, Tiffany, I think I would hate you.' I can remember looking at her in shock and thinking 'wow'. The fact that I was having a potentially serious medical exploration of my heart meant that she liked me more. It made me more 'human' based on her perception of the world and comparison of herself. If I had something 'wrong' with me then we weren't so different after all.

This is the crazy world we have created. Ultimately, I was diagnosed with a heart condition, put on beta blockers and salt tablets and told that I would have this condition for the rest of my life and that it was degenerative. Luckily for me, my personal journey that has led me to writing this today ensured that I didn't believe in my diagnosis and I stopped all of the medication with no ill effects when I was 27.

The point is that having this 'condition' served me. It made me imperfect and people liked me more. They also wanted to look after me and you can't bully someone with a heart condition, right? There are lots of reasons why I created this situation, all of which were subconscious and I only see clearly now with the benefit of hindsight and awareness. As soon as I didn't need the condition anymore, I stopped having it. That is the power of our beliefs. So why didn't I need it anymore? I had moved to Asia as a young, female manager in the region and I needed to be strong. I needed to be more masculine to survive and thrive in such a male dominated industry and culture. Or at least that was what I thought. We are an amazingly adaptable species which is why we are at the top of the food chain; we are chameleons of change absorbing what we believe our environments want from us and finding creative ways to fit in.

Eventually, I learned through my time in Asia that it was my unique individuality that allowed me to thrive. It was questioning everything that I was told was impossible and finding creative ways to make these things possible that enabled me to find success where others hadn't. Trying to be like them meant that I made the same decisions in the same way. Einstein's theory of Insanity is "Doing the same thing in the same way and expecting different results." Our diversity and differences create new, fresh ways of thinking leading to creativity and innovation.

Going back to the concept of do we really see ourselves, the answer is no. We see a perception of self-based on our patterns and beliefs, on what we have already experienced that day, week, month and year, and also based on the projection of how we think other people see us. It is a complicated lens to look through and one which does not reflect how other people see us.

This does mean however that we can change our perception of self both now and what we have perceived in the past. To do this we need to first become aware of the patterns and beliefs we are running that are affecting how we feel about ourselves.

For example, for the majority of my adult life I had a debilitating fear of public speaking. I would almost say that it had become a phobia. I loved to facilitate groups and thrived in that environment but give me an opportunity to stand up on a stage in front of a large group of people with a microphone and all of my knowledge disappeared. My knees would literally start knocking together, my mouth would go dry and I would freeze. Time and time again I tried to 'face my fear' and 'get over' how I felt but nothing changed. I know now that this is because I was using short term coping mechanisms but I will cover that later.

Without going into too much detail here, three years ago I started a process of releasing from my fear by understanding that it was created from a self-limiting belief that I didn't have anything interesting to say. With hindsight I know now that this fear served me as I wasn't ready to get up and speak and that I could more easily clear from it when I felt strongly that I had a message to share and that I really wanted to share it.

From the moment that I started to clear, I energetically broadcast out to the world that I was ready to speak and opportunities started to effortlessly flood in. What I mean by energetically broadcast is that I believe we are all made up of energy and our thoughts and beliefs are a frequency of that energy that are broadcast out from us like radio signals that other people can tune into. Meaning that no matter what persona you are using or how 'brave' you are being, people can feel your frequency and without understanding how or why, have a subconscious knowing of how you are feeling.

So, I start the process of clearing from my fear of public speaking, I feel curious about the fact that I feel more neutral about being given an opportunity to speak, in fact I feel like I might want to try it. This gets broadcast out and before I know it, I get a call from TEDx in Delhi asking me if I will go and do a talk, which I do. I almost don't as when I am standing waiting to go on stage some of my old fears surface and I know I still have work to do but despite the enormous urge to flee, I walk onto stage and deliver my first professional talk.

I couldn't even think about watching afterwards and I cringe as I think about what a terrible job I did. This immediate perception of myself was distorted and based on the fear that surfaced just before I spoke. I was angry with myself for feeling the fear and so in that moment couldn't learn what created it.

After many people sought me out to congratulate me on both my topic and delivery, I began to feel curious about it. Perhaps it wasn't as bad as I thought it was. When I actually got around to watching it, I could see my nerves but I was proud of myself and surprised at how well I had come across.

Before I could learn from this experience, I was contacted by BOLD Talks which is a speaker event, based in the UAE. They asked me if I would come and speak about The Business Case for Women in Leadership in Dubai and again, I said yes. Having met the organisers I was also asked to MC the whole day which meant staying on stage and introducing all of the other speakers before finally speaking myself. Again, I said yes.

On the actual day, I felt anxious and could definitely feel my stress levels going up, the fear was still there but smaller. I had to use will power to stand up on the stage and by the time I delivered my talk at the end of the day my perception of self was really low. All of the other speakers had been authentic, brilliant and inspiring. How could I be the final speaker following all of that?

This goes back to how we compare ourselves based on our perception of others. Since that talk I discovered that many of the speakers were nervous and didn't want to watch their talks after. I was so engrossed in my own fear and limiting belief that I didn't see that we were all pushing our comfort zones and doing something out of the ordinary.

After my talk I went and hid, reduced to tears and promising myself that I wouldn't 'put myself through that again'. I saw it as a 'bad' experience rather than something to learn from and it had to be louder than the TEDx experience because I hadn't learned that time.

Again, after some great feedback I became curious about my talk and could watch it. The feedback had given me confidence and therefore my perception had changed. As I watched I could see many ways to make my talk better and there were a lot of 'ums' but I could be proud of myself for doing it.

This time I really wanted to learn from the experience so I could clear more of my stuff that was creating the fear. My partner who had facilitated my clearing on this whole journey helped me to understand that I couldn't compare the two talks and that by MC'ing the BOLD Talk I was stepping even further out of my comfort zone before I had even got used to speaking. He showed me that it was incredible that I had said yes and not only did my fear come from not having anything to say but I was also running a pattern of being perfect.

If I was going to stand up and speak, I wanted it to be perfect straight away. I wanted to be funny, fast paced and dynamic just like the others speakers I admired. This is another example of comparing ourselves to others and creating unrealistic expectations rather than just being ourselves. I knew by the time I did BOLD Talks that I had something I wanted to say but I was putting myself under pressure by wanting to deliver it in a 'perfect' way.

As I had this realisation, I was contacted by TEDx in Haneda, Japan and asked if I would come and give a talk which I did. Think about how amazing this is for a minute. I had gone from a phobia of speaking to doing three professional, filmed talks in three countries in the space of six months. That is how quickly we can clear from our stuff if we are in a learning mindset.

This third talk was me stepping even further out of my comfort zone as I was delivering to an audience of non-native English speakers and I had to speak slow enough for the translators to do their job which meant that I found it difficult to keep to my flow. I actually learned my talk off by heart which allowed me to remember where I was even if I lost concentration but means that the talk sounds like I am reading a speech.

There was a hilarious part of the talk which has been edited out of the video clip where I mean to say 'bigger, better, faster, stronger' and what actually comes out of my mouth is 'bigger bastards' which made me laugh, eased my tension and allowed me to find a much more natural flow. This 'mistake' showed my vulnerability, that I was human and I could feel the audience in that moment wanting me to do well and I did.

Four years on, I have now found my natural flow with speaking. I know that I have something interesting to say and I deliver it in a way that is authentically me. I can also watch my talks and immediately see what I like in them and what I would like to do differently next time but this is a gentle developmental process, not a destructive criticism that what I have done is 'bad'. I am firmly in the learning mindset and I understand that if I say or don't say something, or I say it in a specific way, then that is what was meant to happen for me and for the audience.

My awareness of self is growing every day and therefore my perception is constantly changing and I am realising just how beautifully unique we are and that this is much more interesting than trying to all be the same.

Homework:

Spend two minutes sitting in front of a mirror looking at yourself without doing anything else. No brushing your teeth or hair, no plucking or grooming. Just look at yourself. Notice what comes up for you. Is it easy? Does it feel like a short or long time? What do you notice about yourself? Write everything down after you have gone through the process.

What can you learn about yourself from this process? Did you immediately notice the things that you don't like about yourself? Were you critical of what you saw in yourself?

How do you think this reflects how you feel about yourself internally?

We can always find time to sit with a friend and spend time listening and noticing what is going on for them but we rarely give this gift to ourselves. By spending two minutes looking at yourself every day you will be able to check in with how you are feeling and also become more comfortable with who you are and how you look.

If you have a significant other or a loved one that you would like to involve in this process, spend two minutes looking at each other without speaking. Feedback what you notice afterwards and share the insights that come to you. In our busy world we are often like passing ships in the night and spending just two minutes to really see each other can open up conversations and realisations that need to be had.

You can also recreate this process with friends by inviting to spend some time together and after 30 minutes putting them into pairs and asking each person to write down on paper how they think they showed up today. How did they look and how did they come across? Then ask them to write the same for their partner. How do they think their partner showed up today? After they have finished writing they can share with each other and notice what is different. It is a lovely way of demonstrating how distorted our self-perception can be and helping the people in your eco-system to become more aware of their fears and limiting beliefs which is the first step to clearing from them.

Notice what is different, not what is the same.

Self-Fulfilling Prophecies
The Power of Our Beliefs

Our beliefs are the most powerful things we have. They shape our decisions and choices; they define how we perceive ourselves and others and they create the world that we live in. The interesting thing about our beliefs is that we think we know what they are but once you understand that we have both a conscious and subconscious mind you begin to see that we have belief systems running that we aren't even aware of that are affecting who we are and what we do.

Our conscious mind is the rationale, logical part of us. It is what we know that we know. If someone asks me what my name is or where I live, I am accessing my conscious mind to find this information. Our subconscious is what we don't know that we know. It not only contains all of the information we have ever received it also contains information from our heritage, genes and from the experiences of our ancestors. Our subconscious remembers everything we have ever seen, felt, heard, smelled, experienced, read and said. This is too much information for our conscious mind to filter through every day so we file it away in our subconscious.

What this means is that we can be running patterns of behaviour based on beliefs that are in our subconscious that we aren't fully aware of. Let's say for example that when I was younger, I saw a person from another country be extremely rude to someone else, I might create a belief that all people from that country are rude. Years later when I come across someone from that country, I am expecting them to be rude but I don't consciously know this. If I interact with that person or observe them, I am looking for confirmation of this sub-conscious belief so that I know that I am correct.

It becomes a self-fulfilling prophecy. If I am subconsciously broadcasting out that all people from that country are rude, I am much more likely to attract in an experience that confirms this belief. If someone then suggested that I was racist my conscious mind would deny that this is true because the belief is in my subconscious, although it may resonate on some level.

My experience has been that we are amazing at creating experiences to confirm our belief systems regardless of whether we are aware of them or not. Another example would be if I was running a subconscious belief that I am not good enough and that no one in my family is ever successful. I could have an opportunity for a promotion and my conscious mind believes that I deserve it and is telling me all of the right things to do to get the promotion. On paper I have exceeded my targets and I have all of the skills and qualifications to step into the new role so in theory receiving the promotion should be relatively easy but when I meet with my boss, I subconsciously do something that shows that I am not good enough for the job. My alarm clock might not go off on that particular morning so I am late to the meeting, or I suddenly develop a cold the night before or during the meeting I am saying all of the right things but my boss can feel my broadcast that I am not good enough and this creates enough doubt for me not to get the promotion.

When this happens, I have two choices, I can either walk away from the meeting or blame my boss or myself, or I can step into a learning mindset and ask myself why I created not getting the promotion. Being able to understand that I have a belief that I am not good enough allows me to decide whether this belief is still serving me or not? Do I really want the promotion or even to stay in the company or country? If it is not serving me anymore then it is time to start a process of clearing.

This is what happened with my fear of public speaking. It served me for a while because I wasn't ready to speak and then when it didn't anymore and I really wanted to get my message out there I was ready to start the process of releasing from my fear.

Being in a blame mindset 'my boss doesn't like me anyway; I would never get the promotion' doesn't help you to learn anything. It is also disempowering as it puts all of the emphasis on and gives power to the boss. He/she did that to me. This is the same if you are blaming yourself 'I should have got up early, I should have prepared more, I should have…' There is no downside to thinking that a subconscious belief has become a self-fulfilling prophecy (created your reality), as it means that you have the power to change it.

So how do we become aware of these subconscious beliefs so that we are able to clear from them? The first step is to be aware of when you are blaming and know that this is stopping you from learning. As much as I possibly can, I take 100% responsibility for everything I am creating in my world. The easiest thing for us to do is blame. A good example of this is with a lady that I was working with who had a string of 'bad' bosses. She kept quitting her jobs because her bosses were so mean to her and each time, she started a new job she expected her boss to be mean. She was running a subconscious belief that she wasn't good enough and so created work experiences where her boss would mirror this back to her.

Blaming her boss and moving company was stopping her from learning why she was creating these experiences. She was in a victim mindset and not realising that the common denominator each time she moved was herself. Our friends often help us to stay in the victim mindset by feeding our story ('my boss is so mean to me', 'yes you poor thing your boss sounds horrible') rather than asking us what we could be doing to create so many 'mean' bosses.

The moment she stopped blaming her boss, she started the process of clearing and we could explore why she was creating the situation. By asking herself 'what is this teaching me', she entered a mindset where she could realise that being a stay at home mum for years had knocked her confidence and she didn't think she was good enough to be doing the job that she was doing. Also, as we explored deeper, she realised that actually she didn't want to work for anyone else, she wanted to set up her own business but her belief that she wasn't good enough was stopping her from doing that.

In this scenario, the bosses that she was creating were fulfilling their roles perfectly to mirror her beliefs back to her and also provide her with the impetus and courage to leave and do something for herself.

The process of clearing for this lady was to stop blaming and take responsibility for what she was creating, to ask what she can learn from the experience and ultimately find out how the belief she is running is serving her and whether is still needs to.

We also use imagination, creativity and play as ways to access our subconscious and clear from fears and self-limiting beliefs but I will come onto that later. For now, it is enough to understand that our beliefs are creating our reality, that they are or have been serving us in some way and that once we learn why we have them we can clear from them or change them which in turn changes the reality we are living in.

Another great example of how powerful our beliefs are is when we look at evidence related to the placebo and nocebo effects. The placebo effect is where a group of participants in a medical trial are either given a real drug or a sugar pill and all told that the pill will make them better. No one knows whether they have the real drug or the sugar pill and all of them make significant improvements in health or are cured. This has been proven time and time again to be true – just search placebo effect in google and you will see hundreds if not thousands of examples.

The nocebo effect is even more interesting as it is a similar scenario but instead of saying that the pill will make you better, the researchers tell you that it will make you ill. There is a great example where everyone in the trial was told that they would experience hair loss as a result of taking the drug and everyone did. It is amazing to think that the power of our beliefs can actually make our hair fall out.

If you are interested in this subject, I suggest you look into people with dissociative identity disorder and how powerful their beliefs are. There are examples of individuals whose eye colour changes depending on which personality they are. There are cases where one personality has diabetes or high cholesterol and the others don't, where one personality is blind and another can see. I find this very exciting as it demonstrates the true potential we have as human beings. These cases show that our beliefs can be so powerful that they can physically and genetically change us from one minute to the next.

Up until 1954, no one believed that a human could run a mile in four minutes or under. Thousands of people tried and failed. It took until Roger Bannister finally broke the world record and ran the mile in four minutes that everyone's belief system changed and suddenly lots of people could.

Why can't we heal ourselves or fly? Maybe because we don't currently believe that we can. Could it be that the potential of the human is only limited by our beliefs?

We can see that these limiting beliefs have served us as a race in that we are now extremely technologically and medically advanced. We can do amazing things but who is to say that we couldn't have done these things anyway with the power of our minds? Does having sci-fi like prosthetic limbs mean that we will never step into the possibility that we can regrow our own? Does the internet and virtual communication mean that we will never be able to communicate telepathically as a race?

There are so many stories of people who have been told that they will never walk again or that they only have a few weeks left to live and because they haven't believed it to be true, they have become 'medical miracles' and proved the doctors wrong. There are also examples of people who have been misdiagnosed and told that they have a fatal disease which ultimately led to their death.

Our beliefs become self-fulfilling prophecies that impact our lives and our ecosystems. There is absolutely no downside to believing that anything is possible or to understanding that we have subconscious beliefs that we don't know we are running which are affecting us every single day.

I am still on my journey of learning what these beliefs are and clearing from the ones that no longer serve me and my life is getting more and more effortless as I do.

Launching RoundTable Global as a brand-new organisation is a great example of this effortlessness. Before we started operating in March 2015, my co-founders and I took time to agree on the kind of organisation that we wanted to create. We wanted it to be different from all of the other companies we knew and to break all of the rules in terms of corporate belief systems around what is possible.

First of all, we decided that we wanted work to be effortless and to be able to create a working environment where everyone was fulfilling their passions at the same time as making a difference in the world. We decided not to create a strategy for the organisation as we felt that this would limit our beliefs around what is possible and we also agreed that we would create an organisation where our commercial programmes would not only fund fantastic lifestyles and travel for us all, it would also fund our philanthropic aims to give back.

We didn't listen to or believe in the well-known advice out there that was telling us that all new start-ups take at least a year to make money, or that you have to fail to succeed or make mistakes to learn.

We fundamentally believed that we could make money straight away (which we did), that we would effortlessly attract business and contributors in (which we also did) and that there is no such thing as mistakes, only opportunities to learn.

The business advice out there, especially from well know entrepreneurs who are extremely successful creates a belief system and mindset that starting your own business is going to be hard work and if you believe that to be true, guess what you create? A self-fulfilling prophecy of hard work, failure and 'mistakes'. In fact, lots of start-up businesses fail before the end of year one and I am certain it is down to this advice.

We found that the exact opposite was true. By genuinely believing that we create our world through our beliefs and that life can be effortless we have a launched a truly global organisation that is delivering the lifestyle and good in the world that we are all passionate about and we are in a position to self-fund absolutely everything we do.

In fact I am sitting in the mountains in Bali writing this chapter and have just learned that we have won an International Business Award 'Changing the World is our Responsibility' as Start-up of the Year which is fantastic recognition given that we are such a small and young organisation and over 3800 companies from around the world were nominated.

Who would have believed that this was possible? Well, we did. We are extremely excited about winning the award but we are also not surprised. This month we have also been shortlisted for three other national awards which again most start-ups would not believe is possible.

There are so many other examples of how we have challenged what is currently believed to be true in the business and specifically consulting/development world such as when you work with a large multinational you have to adhere to their payment terms. This can sometimes be as much as 90 days which makes it very difficult for small suppliers to survive as it creates cash flow issues. With all of our clients we have negotiated either payment before delivery or payment terms that are all within 30-days of delivery. We did this by believing that what we offer is powerful enough that organisations will be flexible to ensure that they can work with us.

We also created payment terms which describe how our cash flow is used to fund our philanthropic initiatives and that by paying within our terms, clients will be helping us to continue to do good in the world and therefore be more socially responsible themselves. It has a knock-on feel-good factor which works.

We have questioned everything we knew to be true about the business world and leadership development industry and created new beliefs around what is possible. These beliefs are now being adopted by other entrepreneurs that we are working with as they can see that they are true.

Why would you believe that you have to make mistakes to learn or fail to succeed when you can make choices that help you to learn without seeing them as bad things that have happened and that you can be successful without having to fail? This belief system and mindset change has created a much more effortless and stress-free way of living and working than I could have ever imagined.

Homework:

Spend time writing down the things in your life that you are not happy with or that you would like to change. Think about how and why you have created them. How have they served you? What is the learning? As you ask yourself these questions do you become aware of any fears or beliefs that could be creating the situations? Do you have any self-limiting beliefs? You don't need to understand where the beliefs have come from just that they are there and impacting your life.

Are you reading books, watching documentaries or listening to coaches and mentors that are feeding your limiting beliefs about what is possible? Listen to what they are teaching you and ask yourself if this is creating even more limiting beliefs.

Notice what is different, not what is the same.

The Creative Learning Mindset

Do you believe that everything happens for a reason? If you really believe it you will be in the mindset that there is no such thing as a mistake or failure. How do you feel about that? The very concept of a mistake means that it wasn't meant to happen, same for failure. I am 100% in the mindset that absolutely everything happens for a reason and that anything that doesn't go the way I expected it to is an opportunity to learn and will take me on a different path which could be even more exciting and interesting.

If I am at an airport and my flight is delayed or cancelled, there is absolutely no part of me that gets anxious, stressed or angry, regardless of where the plane was taking me or what I was meant to be doing. I am just curious. Curious to discover who I might meet while I have longer at the airport, who I might bump into at the other end that I never would have met otherwise, what I might have encountered if I had been on time… you get the picture. I know that there will be a reason for it happening and this allows me to enjoy what unfolds as a result.

I am not saying that I believe in fate by the way, I think we have choices and decisions that we make along the way that influence where we go and what we do but I do believe that we create our world and that all of those choices and decisions lead to things that happen for us to learn.

By saying that I believe everything happens for a reason, I am also saying that I don't believe that anything is random. If I sneeze now, I stop and ask myself what I was thinking about. We sneeze because of irritation so was there something that was irritating me at the time? If someone bumps into me making me stop, I look up and scan to see if there is something that I am supposed to see that I wouldn't have otherwise. If my leg starts to hurt, I will stop and ask myself what it is teaching me. I have a great example of when this actually happened.

I was in Waterloo station in London meeting one of my co-founders, Charlotte for breakfast. I had a full day of meetings lined up and I was feeling good despite having just delivered a number of programmes back to back in multiple countries. As we started to walk up the stairs to the cafe my knee buckled and was excruciatingly painful so much so that I couldn't put any weight on it and Charlotte had to help me up the steps. Because of the mindset I am in, at the top of the steps I stopped and asked myself what my knee was teaching me. First of all, I go to what it could prevent me from doing and then I ask what it enables me to do. The answers were obvious, not being able to walk meant that I couldn't do my meetings that day and could return home, guilt-free, for a day of rest which I immediately decided to do.

In the Uber, on my way home, my knee was still painful and I messaged all of the people I was due to meet and explained the situation, at no point did I apologise because I am also of the mindset that we co-create everything. I had created this pain so I could rest and also potentially because we weren't ready to meet yet and they had also created it for their own reasons. Knowing this takes away so much stress from life. We spend so much of our time feeling guilty about things and worrying about letting other people down that we don't prioritise our own health and happiness. What I am discovering more and more is that by prioritising yourself you have abundance to give to others.

When I arrived home, I still couldn't put weight on my knee although it was feeling a bit better and the moment I stepped over the threshold home, the pain completely disappeared.

That is how amazing our bodies are at showing us what we need. Now the old me would have told myself to 'man up' and taken painkillers so that I could push on through, potentially resulting in an injury. The old me also would have felt the pain leave my knee and then gone straight back out again. The feeling of guilt and worry being stronger that my own sense of wellbeing. I have never had an injury in that knee and nothing happened to create the pain, it was just suddenly there and by listening to it and making a new choice, it disappeared.

I have so many examples of this happening on our programmes where someone checks in in the morning with excruciating pain somewhere in their bodies and by the end of the day having worked through what is going on from them it is completely gone.

One lady I worked with recently on a Shine Programme in London arrived on the morning of day two with a swollen and sore foot, so much so that she was feeling stressed and in a 'bad place'. From her perspective nothing had happened to cause the pain and even the pain killers she had been taking weren't touching the sides. During the break I asked her if she wanted me to help her with it and she sceptically agreed. I asked her what had happened that evening and after some questioning from me I discovered that she had an argument with her sister. I asked her how she felt about the argument and she said that she was frustrated because they were supposed to be booking a trip to go on holiday together and her sister wouldn't commit to anything and was holding her back.

I could tell straight away that this was causing the pain in her foot. I asked her if she could see that in her mind her sister was stopping her from moving forward with the trip and she said yes. I asked her to try walking and she told me that the pain had lessened but was still there. So, I asked her if there was anything else that she wanted to say. She told me that she felt like her sister was always letting her down and that she had to do everything, that she had spent hours and hours looking into the holiday and felt like 'she had run a marathon with no benefits.' I repeated back to her what she had just said and then said 'no wonder your foot is hurting!' We both laughed and when she walked around again the pain was even less. I talked to her about the fact that the anger was coming from blaming her sister for stopping her from booking the holiday and we discussed the fact that this was a pattern between the siblings. Eventually we got to a realisation that she was setting huge expectations for her sister to be the same as her which meant that her sister was constantly letting her down which put them both in an angry/blame mindset. My participant was holding her sister in a pattern of letting her down and so creating situations where she could show that she was right.

The sister was fulfilling her role perfectly. It doesn't matter during this kind of conversation why the sister was creating it (perhaps she had a belief that being the younger sister meant that she wasn't as good as her sibling) all that mattered was that my participant realised that she could take responsibility for her part in the creation, stop holding her sister in the pattern of letting her down and go ahead and book the holiday for both of them. It is always exciting for me to watch the realisations come and to see the stress and anger change to amusement and curiosity. The next time she walked around the pain was completely gone. This whole process took about ten minutes and no painkillers were needed.

If we hadn't have gone through that process and she hadn't have stepped into a learning mindset, the message (the pain) would have had to get louder and louder until she eventually learned.

To reiterate, absolutely everything that happens is for a reason and to learn from and life can be so much more effortless (and painless) when you embrace this way of living.

I do want to mention that when I went through this process, I spent a lot of my time trying to work out why the other person created the situation which is a really frustrating. It can also put you in a blame mindset so that you don't learn. The most authentic and empowering thing you can do in any situation is to take 100% responsibility for your part in the creation and ask yourself what you can learn from it. This also takes the heat out of potential altercations because if you are not blaming you are not angry and if you are trying to learn from the situation you aren't 'in the story' of what has happened or is happening.

It is also important to be aware if you are blaming yourself as this is still blaming and was also something I did at the beginning. I would get stuck in asking myself why I had created something and be frustrated that I didn't have an answer. What I have learned now is, ask yourself the question but don't be attached to getting an answer. Just understanding that you have co-created a situation changes your experience of it. Knowing that you have created it for a reason takes you even further into a place where realisations and learning can come.

Let's return to my statement about believing that nothing is random. Lots of the people I have worked with find this a challenging concept to grasp, especially when I follow it by saying that I don't believe in fate. However, once we start exploring synchronicity stories, their minds start to change. Synchronicity is a concept, first introduced by analytical psychologist Carl Jung, which holds that events are "Meaningful coincidences," if they occur with no causal relationship yet seem to be meaningfully related. Absolutely everyone I have met has an amazing synchronistic story. Something that had happened that just can't be random or a coincidence and the more you explore these stories, the more you can see how beautifully connected we all are.

One of my most breath-taking synchronicity stories happened in Goa in India. For 13 years, my parents owned a bijoux hotel in Palolem and most years my sisters and I went to visit them. This particular year I had convinced a whole group of my friends to go with me which I was very excited about. Before we left, I had started to research educational reform and what we need to do to really unlock potential and tap into skills and talents of the future generation which is one of my passions in life. Because she was aware of this, an elderly relative of my then husband gave me an article to read about an Argentinian family who had adapted a car to be usable as a place to travel and sleep and taken off around the world to explore and write. During the following 12 years, they had three children who were on the road with them, had been born in different countries and were being 'home' schooled whilst on their travels.

I was intrigued to know what these children were like without access to traditional education and instead learning through their experiences and connection to multiple cultures and people.

The article had been written many months before and at that time the family were traveling through Russia. I made a mental note to try and connect with them through their blog after my holiday and took the article with me to show to my mum.

Another intriguing thing about their story was that they only ever stayed for one to two nights in any place that they stopped in.

One morning while we were in Goa, the majority of my friends woke up with sickness and diarrhoea because they had eaten meat at one of the beach restaurants. Having been a vegetarian for the majority of my life I was one of the only ones that were OK and during breakfast had a chance to tell my mum about the Argentinian family.

We had planned a trip that day but as everyone felt so sick, we cancelled it and my mum convinced me instead to go and have a picnic with her on a beach that was half an hour away. We cooked far too much food while we were there and as we were deciding what to do with it a car drove onto the beach. My mum spotted it first and realised immediately that it was the Argentinian family. They had driven onto the beach that we weren't meant to be on at exactly the time that we wanted to share our food, it was astonishing and perfect.

The family were quite surprised when we approached them to eat with us and I knew all of their names, but as I told them the story they laughed and said that this kind of thing happened all the time with them. That they were very much in the flow and knowing that where ever they ended up was where they were meant to be. We sat and ate and I had a chance to speak to the children about their experiences which inspired me to create some of the work we are doing now around educational reform.

When we returned to the hotel to tell my friends, all of whom knew about the article, they couldn't quite believe us until we showed them the photographs. The chances of us meeting that family were so slim that they were almost impossible. There was nothing random about us meeting and that is how amazing the world is.

In this example with the benefit of hindsight, the 'bad situation' which was my friends all getting ill happened so that I could go to a different beach with my mum at exactly the right time to meet with the family. It happened for a reason.

Understanding the power of synchronicity rather than thinking that things are random, also helps you to learn, change and grow more quickly.

There are many things that happen in our lives that catalyse change like going off on an adventure, getting married, losing someone, losing a job or even just deciding to cycle to work every day rather than take the train. When these things happen, we often go into a heightened state of emotion, especially if the change is something that we see as bad. Let's say for example losing someone. This means that the grieving and healing process can take a very long time, especially as we believe that there are 'stages of grief that everyone goes through', meaning that we are constantly looking to create the next stage rather than go through the process in our own unique way.

The timeline for this process really does depend on how you view the loss. Of course, it is our preference to not lose anyone in our lives but people do die and sometimes in the most extreme circumstances. Being in a mindset of blame and anger, stops the healing and learning process. With the benefit of hindsight, there is always a reason for why this change has happened.

A few years ago, a very close friend of my family took his own life by jumping in front of a train which was extremely traumatic for everyone involved from the train driver to his girlfriend and family. I was told the news while at an internal team meeting in Thailand and I was of course devastated. The emotions we feel in these situations are valid and human, I am not saying that we shouldn't feel anything. However, many of the people that knew him were angry that he had committed such a selfish act but I felt strongly that if he needed to leave that badly then it was his decision to make. I also knew because of the journey I am on that there would be a reason for him leaving for each of us, in that our lives would not be the same because of this loss.

He had actually reached out to me a few months before he died, saying that it would be great to meet up and that he really needed to talk but I had been busy globe-trotting and didn't make the time to see him. When I found out that he had taken his own life I instantly felt guilty about this and wished that things had been different. Once I got through the initial shock and sadness, I then started to think about all of my other relationships and friendships, especially the people that I hadn't seen for a long time and I realised that nothing is more important than our connection with others. His passing meant that I re-evaluated what was important to me and made significant changes in my life as part of this process.

Being grateful to him for teaching me this allowed me to work through my grief much quicker than I would have otherwise and also meant that I wasn't stuck in a place of anger or blame.

To reiterate, would I have stopped him from jumping in front of a train if I could? Absolutely, but the fact is that he did it and the only thing I can change is my perception of what happened by realising and being grateful for what it taught me. I now see my relationship with myself and others as far more important than wealth and success.

Notice what is different, not what is the same.

What Are You Broadcasting?

We are energetic beings and this energy is much larger than our physical bodies. Where ever we go we are broadcasting emotions, thoughts and feelings out from us like pheromones. As energetic beings this also means that we feel each other, meaning that we can feel and interpret what is being broadcast without ever touching the other person.

Take for example, when a speaker walks onto the stage with a huge smile on their face and you just know that they are nervous. How do you know this? They haven't spoken yet; they haven't given any indication that they are nervous but you just know. It is because you can feel the nerves coming from them and depending on your beliefs or what patterns you are running you will interpret this and decide how to act accordingly. If you have a fear of speaking yourself you will probably empathise and want them to succeed. If you are a client that has paid a lot of money for this talk and you have a belief that you can do a better job yourself you will probably want them to show their nerves. Both of which they will feel back from you and depending on their beliefs and patterns this will then affect their perception of themselves and have an impact on their performance.

I am sure you have all experienced someone who is in sales who is trying to convince you to buy something and is saying all of the right things in terms of it being the last one available, or having a discount that will soon run out. They are smiling and acting confidently but you just know that they absolutely need you to purchase. You can feel their desperation and it affects your decision as to whether to buy or not.

Another example relevant to me is when at the age of 26 I moved to Asia in a management role for my previous company and I would go into meetings with an older male consultant who I was training. I know now that at times I entered the room feeling my age with a belief system that I was too young to be doing what I was doing and to be taken seriously. Even though I was acting professionally and confidently, the client would feel me broadcasting this belief and would more often than not assume that I was the assistant or note taker, focusing all of their energy on my colleague. I would then feel this lack of confidence in me and maybe a subconscious bias from them that I was a young woman in a man's world and my performance would be limited.

Being aware of what you are broadcasting helps you to understand how you are creating self-fulfilling prophecies and how to change this. What we broadcast out, we attract in. Another example would be if we feel like we are having a bad day. Everything in our being is either resigned to the fact that this is going to be a bad day or is angry about that fact so the energy we are broadcasting out is either victim or anger. If this is the case then the experiences, we are likely to attract in will fulfil our belief that bad things are going to happen all day (can't get a taxi, lose all my emails, leave my umbrella on the train) and/or make us even angrier.

In this heightened emotional state, you will notice other people in a similar state and attract each other like magnets to fulfil the prophecy. For example, if you are angry in this bad day scenario and someone jumps in front of you in a queue, if they are in a victim mindset you will feel pulled in to shout at them. If you are in a victim mindset in this scenario you will feel like that person has bullied you and will spiral even further into feelings of stress or anxiety.

This concept of having a bad day is ingrained into our culture and is an acceptable excuse for blaming other people, situations or blaming yourself. Let's say that this bad day started with the alarm clock not waking you up on time which caused you to rush, burn breakfast, spill coffee on your shirt, miss the train and end up having to run to work in the rain. At what point are you going to learn that you are not supposed to arrive at work on time that day? When you enter your work building soaking wet and depressed or angry? Or as soon as you wake up and notice that the alarm hasn't gone off? If it is when you enter the building then you have already broadcast out and attracted in five additional experiences to teach you this (rush, burn breakfast, spill coffee, miss train, run in the rain). If it is when you wake up and you think to yourself 'I wonder why I am not supposed to arrive at work in time today' not only will you save yourself a lot of stress and emotion but you will enter into a solution driven mindset and be broadcasting this out to the world.

Knowing that you create your world and that everything is to learn from, helps you see that nothing you are creating is bad and that with the benefit of hindsight there is always a reason why that thing happened. In this bad day example it might be that being late means you bump into someone that has the potential to change your life, or that when you arrive in victim or angry your boss responds in such a way that it is the catalyst for you leaving which is something you really wanted to do but were too fearful of doing.

You are broadcasting out and attracting in the very things that you need to learn and change. Nothing in your life is there to derail you, it is all beautifully created to help you, even if it doesn't feel like it is at the time.

Our subconscious perceptions of self-act as a broadcast centre which effects the people around us and through this, we are constantly teaching them how to treat us. If we are in a victim mindset because we have a belief that nothing is ever easy for us or we feel insecure about our age/gender/ethnicity/experience etc. we will attract in behaviour that mirrors these beliefs back to us. We will pull in people or experiences where we can each play our role perfectly. A victim will pull in a bully or another victim which will either feed our story or help us to learn. The people who you have the most conflict with are usually our best teachers. They can show us how we see ourselves, what patterns we are running and what our belief systems are.

Often when we come across someone that we don't like we either see something in them that reminds us of ourselves or of a fear that we have about being like that. It can also be because we have a subconscious belief running about that type of person. Either way, it is an opportunity to learn and by stopping and asking ourselves what it is about them that is triggering us we stop blaming, change our energy and perception and start to learn.

How many times a day do you say the word sorry? I used to have 'sorry Tourettes' and would apologise to people and inanimate objects that I bumped into hundreds of times a day. When you realise that the word sorry can be translated into 'I made a mistake' or 'I did something wrong' you realise what an impact this can have on your confidence and your well-being.

Before I understood that everything happens to learn from, I had a belief that arriving somewhere late was unprofessional and unacceptable. I used to get extremely stressed on my way to meetings if something out of my control happened and I was going to be late. I would immediately send the person waiting a message to say sorry and I would arrive in an apologetic state. This would teach the person waiting that I felt I had done something wrong and pull them into react in an appropriate way which would be to feel disappointed, angry or put out in some way.

I believe that in any interaction with another person, energetically speaking there is always only space for 100% between us. Meaning that is one person is giving 60% energy (contribution/participation etc.) the other person can only give 40%. In a 'being late' scenario where you arrive apologising, you are immediately putting yourself in a 20-40% position which means that the other person has to step into 60-80% and they do this by demonstrating authority in the situation. You are on the back foot and have to work hard to make up some of that lost percentage.

Once I realised all of this, I spent some weeks eradicating the word sorry from my vocabulary and as much as is humanly possible I no longer apologise for anything that happens. The reason for this is that I fundamentally know that anything that happens outside of my control is being co-created for a bigger picture reason and also because I don't believe that anything is a mistake. Of course, if I stand on someone's foot on the tube, I might feel like I want to say sorry as I don't want to spend time explaining my philosophy on saying sorry and I also don't want to get into an altercation.

Instead of saying sorry I say thank you. If I know I am going to be late for a meeting I will email or call and explain the situation and thank them for their patience. When I arrive, I will thank them for waiting and ask them what they have done with the time and more often than not the person has a reason for being grateful for that gift of time. I hear things like 'I hadn't eaten anything or had chance to have a coffee all day and once I knew you would be later I took some time to refuel' or 'I had a row with my (loved one) this morning which I have been worrying about all day and I just had a chance to call them' or 'I had a deadline to meet and you arriving now has given me a chance to send that email.'

This is how beautifully it all works. First of all, by not entering into a fear driven, apologetic mindset, I am broadcasting out an appreciative, respectful but equal energy allowing us both to remain in 50%. Secondly by knowing that for whatever reason we both needed that time and the conversation we have after is going to be much better and less stressful than it would have been before.

I have also stopped apologising in emails and instead thank people for their patience, for waiting and for their understanding. I have no doubt that whenever I respond and whatever I am sending to them at that point reaches them at exactly the right time for both of us.

I invite you to explore not saying sorry and see how it impacts your life. It has taken so much of the stress from my life and it now feels much more effortless.

Homework:

In addition to exploring the word sorry, how often you and others say it and what it creates, start to really notice how other people are experiencing you. When you walk into a room, what are you broadcasting? Notice how you are feeling and if the interaction you then have with whoever you are with is affected by this. We constantly act as mirrors for each other so noticing what the people in your life are broadcasting is information for you to learn from regarding how you feel about yourself.

Notice what is different, not what is the same.

I am Great
Supportive Competition

Why is it that we find it so difficult to say that we are great at something? Why is it that when we are offered a compliment, we either feel like we have to offer something similar straight back or somehow make less of it? As women, we are particularly good at this. For example, if I say to a friend 'I really like your dress' they immediately feel like they have to tell me how little it cost, that it was given to them or that it is really old rather than just say 'thank you'. They also then tell me something that they like about what I am wearing or how I look that day. Even if it's not necessarily true. There is a feeling that energetically we need to exchange compliments.

Why is this? My experience has been that we become uncomfortable when someone focuses complimentary energy on us because we feel that we don't deserve it and that somehow if we appreciate what has been offered, we will be seen as egotistical or big headed.

When we walk into a room, we are constantly wondering what other people think of us and if we are good enough or if we are being judged in some way. What is funny about this is that everyone in the room is thinking the same, meaning that no one is actually really focusing attention on anyone else except to notice what they like or admire about that person. This is because we are constantly comparing and assessing ourselves against other people in the hope of 'fitting in'.

There is an activity that we run as part of the Shine programme where we ask the group to stand in a circle and think about something that they are great at. We then ask them one by one to step into the circle and share that thing with the group. What happens every single time regardless of gender or culture is that the majority of people first of all choose something that isn't a personal risk to share (cooking, golf etc.) and secondly they are unable to say the words 'I am great at…' even though this is what we have explicitly asked them to do. They say 'I think I am good at…' or even just the thing itself. For example, stepping into the middle of the group and just saying 'cooking'.

There is an air of apprehension before the first-person steps in to see who will set the bar and how they will do it. Often everyone else will follow suit or a more basic version of the first statement. There is a lack of eye contact with the rest of the group and some people mumble the thing they are great at with their heads down while rushing across the circle.

It is really fascinating to observe just how difficult it is for most people to say what they are great at.

Once everyone has had a turn, I ask them what they noticed about the activity. I rarely have a group that even notices that they don't say the words 'I am great at…' They also don't realise that they are all choosing 'safe' things to declare. Things that they believe are less likely to be judged by the group.

Most group discussions then identify the cause of this reticence as lack of confidence in their individual abilities to know whether something is great or not. The word 'great' is subjective and relevant to personal experience. The question is, why does that matter? If you think you are great at something and are able to confidently share this, you will broadcast this confidence out and the people around you are more likely to agree with you.

When you judge yourself, you project this judgement onto others who will feel your lack of confidence and mirror this back to you. It becomes a self-fulfilling prophecy.

This fear of judgement and lack of confidence is not innate, we are not born with it, it is learned. Ask a child under the age of seven what they are great at and they have absolutely no problem listing all the things they are proud of about themselves. In fact, if you ask the same child what they are not good at they often find it difficult to even understand the question.

We are born with limitless potential and unique individual talents. Every time we lift our heads off the pillow in the mornings this is also true, it is only our limiting beliefs and judgement of self that stops us from reaching our full potential. Our subconscious patterns and learned beliefs slowly creep in throughout the day affecting our energy and enthusiasm.

Have you ever woken up in the morning with what you think is a brilliant idea? A no brainer that will change everything and then by the time you go to bed in the evening you have already dismissed it as something that will never work, you will never get buy in for, or you will never be able to achieve?

Everywhere you look there are advertising and marketing campaigns focused on making money and selling products by making us feel that we are not enough. We are so accustomed to living in a society where we are bombarded by imagery of people that are better than us or have more than us to aspire too, that we aren't consciously aware it is happening. What is interesting to note is that these are the overt campaigns, the ones we know about. Imagine how much subliminal messaging our subconscious is taking in on a day to day basis?

The fear of judgement and the desire to fit in are so prevalent in some cultures that we have even created sayings to ensure that no one is too confident or demonstrative of unique ability which stymies creativity and innovation. For example, having spent so many years working in Japan I am very familiar with the saying 'The nail that stands proud, gets hammered down'. What this creates is a reluctance to be or do anything different from everyone else which is Einstein's definition of insanity (doing the same thing over and over again and expecting different results).

How can we expect to evolve to our full potential as a species if we don't celebrate and encourage our unique talents and abilities? Dumbing ourselves down does not serve any purpose to the greater good of the human.

Once I explain all of this to the group, I offer them another opportunity to step into the circle and offer something meaningful that they are great at and it is exciting to see what happens. The first person (usually an extrovert) will step into the middle and with confidence share something that they are particularly proud of about themselves. Something that in theory is a risk. For example, I could step in and say 'I am a great facilitator' or I might take it even further and say 'I am an excellent facilitator'.

This then sets the bar for everyone else to follow and our concept of Supportive Competition comes into play.

Competition is often seen as a negative concept in the business world and in its masculine form it can be. When you are in the mindset of 'I want to win so that you lose' you are in an exclusive space where you are not able to creatively collaborate or collectively build on ideas. This is sometimes necessary but creates a culture where there is a fear of losing and where individual success is prioritised over that of the team or community.

Supportive Competition in comparison is a feminine approach to collective success and working towards becoming the best that you can be at whatever you are doing. It is a mindset of raising the bar (winning) to encourage everyone else to meet you there or to in turn raise the bar further (also winning). This encourages everyone to exceed personal expectations and to be inclusive in their sharing of the knowledge, resources and ideas that allowed them to raise the bar in the first place.

It is a collaborative, solution driven mindset rather than one of fear and exclusivity.

This is especially important in organisations that are driven by sales as it encourages those that are responsible for selling to work together and offer exciting solutions to clients and customers rather than focusing on the amount of revenue they are personally creating.

I have worked with sales teams that actively hide their new ideas from colleagues and will not share materials and resources for fear of them doing better or winning.

A great example of this is when I delivered a strategic leadership programme in Bahrain for a sales manager and his team and we included a bridge building project. The team were separated into smaller groups and told that they needed to build a bridge within 15 minutes that would (a) span the width of the table they were sitting around and (b) be strong enough to hold the weight of an object in the middle. These were the only instructions.

At the front of the room I had provided a pile of materials and resources and after briefing the groups I stepped back to see what would happen. Every group immediately saw this as a competition and rushed to take as much of the resource available as possible. The Manager of the team actually hid materials that his group didn't need from the rest of the team to ensure 'winning'.

Once the bridges were built and we were testing their ability to hold the object, his team also heckled the rest of the groups and laughed at what they had created. This very masculine competitiveness can create a lack of communication, motivation and cohesiveness. If the manager is more focused on winning and being the best, this is the role model that will be created for the rest of the team.

When I pointed out to the groups that at no point had I said that they couldn't all work together or help each other and that I hadn't said it was a competition, they were shocked at their behaviour and what this had created. For the Sales Manager who was participating in a team building activity to become aware that he had wanted the rest of his team to lose and ensured that this was the case, it was a very insightful realisation into the culture he was creating for the team and what needed to change. What is exciting about this is that it only takes one person at the centre of the eco-system to change and it gives permission for everyone else to do the same.

In comparison, I recently delivered the same project for a group of Young Professionals in Egypt as part of a modular programme for SAP which was a fantastic example of Supportive Competition. Not only did the groups share their ideas with each other in terms of structure and design, one of the participants (who was an engineer) then actively gave his time to each group to ensure that their bridges were sound. This created an inclusive energy in the room and they all cheered as each of the bridges passed the weight test.

This created a sense of achievement and camaraderie that they all enjoyed.

Imagine if you could create teams in your organisation based on a foundation of supportive rather than masculine competition, teams that are confident to share what they are great at and utilise these talents to inclusively raise the bar for everyone.

Also, imagine what you will personally be broadcasting if you can authentically share what you are great at with the people in your eco-system and empower them to do the same. This mindset change will not only develop your self-confidence, it will also start to attract in opportunities that you have been blocking with your fears and limiting beliefs.

Homework:

Go somewhere that is beautiful and/or inspiring to you, somewhere you will not be interrupted and where you can truly connect with yourself. For example, if you are an architect this could be a beautiful building designed by someone you admire. I like to be outside with a beautiful view and either have my feet in the grass or in the sand. I also love to be in water and find that this is a great conductor for creative thinking and self-reflection.

Once you are in that space, close your eyes and connect to your body using the same process as the check in. Then still with your eyes closed, ask yourself what you are great at. When you are ready, open your eyes and write down or record as many things as you can think of. Be aware of how this feels in your body and how it affects you emotionally. Does anything come up? If you are struggling you may want to use the imagination exercise and then think about what you are great at.

Ask other people in your eco-system what they think you are great at. Are those things the same or different to yours? Is there anything you are surprised at?

Practice sharing with people the things that you are great at and encouraging them to do the same with you.

Notice what is different, not what is the same.

Leadership Action

Over the past 19 years I have studied and researched into more theories of what leadership is than I can remember. There are a plethora of philosophies and thinking about what it is to be a leader and they are all useful situationally and in terms of providing toolkits for effective communication and for creating and implementing strategies.

However, the thought leadership that has had most impact on me personally and most resonates in terms of the RoundTable philosophies is John Adair's theory of Action Centred Leadership, meaning that leadership is all about a special kind of action rather than a special kind of person. That without action, there is no leadership.

What really resonates about this approach to leadership is that it is inclusive, it means that anyone at any level in an organisation has the ability to step into leadership by demonstrating authentic action which fills a leadership vacuum.

So, for example let's say that I am the lead, facilitating a group with a co-facilitator in the room with me and in the middle of a sentence I stop talking and walk out of the room. This effectively creates a leadership vacuum as I am no longer leading. In traditional hierarchical leadership, everyone would expect my co-facilitator to step up and fill the vacuum as they would be considered to be second in command.

Everyone would notice that I have left the room, some might even be thinking that they should do something about it but in the old paradigm of leadership it would be rare for anyone other than the co-facilitator to step in.

Once you fully understand and embrace the concept of leadership being action, you create an empowered culture where anyone can step into the vacuum without fear of judgement, if they feel that they have value to add to the situation. This value will almost always be solution driven and galvanise either the whole group into action or at least catalyse a resolution.

Inaction can also be considered an act of leadership if the intention is to empower someone else who needs the experience to step into the vacuum. So, in the example of me leaving the room mid-sentence, my co-facilitator and I may have agreed that this would be a great opportunity to see who in the room has the courage to act. By intentionally not stepping into the vacuum to lead the group, they are empowering someone else to do so.

Now, this isn't an excuse not to act as a leader if you are feeling fearful, which rather than being an intention to empower others, it is a coping mechanism for guilt free inaction.

Authentic leaders have the courage to act. They see that something needs to happen and they feel able to do something about it. Regardless of the eventual outcome, this stepping into the vacuum, especially when it is with passion and purpose, inspires others to follow or empowers them to step into the vacuum with their own ideas.

If you think about the majority of famous leaders in the world, it is doubtful that they have attended any kind of leadership training, at least in the early stages of their careers, but they all have in common the absolute courage of conviction around their values and are able to inspire others with passion and purpose.

I am often asked if people are born to be great leaders or if it is something that can be taught and I always go back to the same answer of passion, purpose and action. Of course, some people are born knowing without any doubt what they want to do and are driven towards that from the start but there are other people who develop as inspirational leaders later on in life when their purpose becomes apparent.

A fantastic example of this and hero of mine is Boyan Slat who at the age of 16 and through his passion of diving created The Ocean Clean-up Project, an ambitious project to rid the world's oceans of plastic. Boyan, an aerospace engineering student drop-out, has now created what all of the world's foremost thinkers in marine biology and environmental conservation could not do. He designed and raised funding for a passive system that works with the oceans natural circulating currents and is predicted to not only rid the oceans of plastic within a matter of years, it also uses the plastic cleared to create saleable products that generate revenue for further research and development.

Boyan is now considered a thought leader and inspirational entrepreneur in marine conservation who galvanised 38,000 donors from 160 countries to collaboratively support his project.

He had a passion (diving) which created a sense of purpose (clean oceans with a healthy, plastic free eco-system) and he had the courage to act (The Ocean Clean-up Project).

Another more personal example, which empowered me to step into inclusive leadership action was when I was invited to join the Duke of Edinburgh's Commonwealth Study Tour. The study tour which started in 1956, is an experience for future leaders from the Commonwealth Countries who are tasked with working together to create solutions for global economic and sustainability issues.

It is an opportunity for those nominated and selected to immerse themselves in and provide feedback and ideas for challenges facing our global eco-system.

There is so much I could tell you about the tour I was part of which was focused on the Sustainability of GDP growth in India but that would be a whole other book and you can find out more by watching my TEDx in Delhi on You Tube. Instead I will just share the parts that are relevant to this chapter.

Firstly, at the very beginning of the Study Tour I was put into a group of 15 other future leaders, all representing different Commonwealth countries and we were told that our focus would be in Delhi looking at leadership, infrastructure and inclusivity for GDP growth. I can remember sitting around a table looking at the impressive people in my group feeling much younger and very inexperienced.

Our Indian facilitator presented us with our agenda for the week and we all sat reading it with only a few conversations happening. I was suddenly struck by the realisation that everyone was feeling nervous and that no-one had been in this situation before and therefore had any idea what to do next. There was a very obvious leadership vacuum in the room.

After a while I realised that no-one was going to step into it and so with some trepidation, I told the group that I was working for a learning and development company and asked them if they wanted me to facilitate a session for us all to get to know each other. To my amazement, everyone seemed hugely relieved and agreed profusely. All eyes were on me as the leader, I was providing structure from a place of authenticity and I had the skills to be able to deliver it.

This profound experience where I had suddenly gone from hierarchically the youngest and least experienced leader in the room to the one leading thing starting a journey of having the courage to act which is still serving me today.

Once I had facilitated the session which enabled us to introduce ourselves, why we were there and also our individual skills and talents, I separated us into smaller groups to look at the agenda and feedback our insights. It was immediately obvious to me that the schedule of people we were due to meet during the week would not give us a diverse and inclusive view of the topics we needed to cover. They were all wealthy senior male leaders and policy makers.

The schedule did not include visiting NPO's dealing with the challenges caused by the poverty gap or hearing from low caste, uneducated communities existing in slums without sanitation or access to clean water. How could we draw conclusions and make informed authentic recommendations for change without an understanding of these things at the very least?

I shared this thinking with the group and because of the bond that we had started to form by sharing information about ourselves, we quickly agreed that something needed to change and proposed a complete revision of the schedule to our Indian facilitator which in turn created another leadership vacuum.

Our facilitator was motivated rather than concerned by our enthusiasm to change everything and stepped into the vacuum despite concerns from the organisers to create a new tour for us that was a true representation of what was the current reality in Delhi.

At no point was I nominated or asked to be leader of the group. Rather I noticed that something needed to happen and I stepped into the space without ego and with the desire to facilitate a more effortless experience for all of us, something which my colleagues were both glad of and inspired by. I captured their imaginations and galvanised their support by thinking differently and leveraging my unique talents in that situation.

This small step into leadership action then led me to an experience that had a huge positive impact later on in the tour. Developing my propensity to act as a leader gave me the courage to do something that would truly make a difference.

Before I share that experience with you, I want to set the scene for why this is important. I have had so many conversations with people passionate about change who do not believe that they have the ability to do anything significant. As we discuss some of the biggest issues, we are facing on this planet they say to me 'what can I do?' 'I am only one person' or 'how can just one person make a difference if no one else changes?' and my response to them is – if we all think like that, nothing will ever change.

Our leadership action is like throwing a pebble into water, the ripples continue on until we can no longer see where they are going. We have no idea of how far reaching the butterfly effect of our action is and the impact this can have so let me inspire you with what is possible.

Towards the end of the study tour, a group of us decided to treat ourselves to an expensive meal in a part of Delhi where the higher castes socialise. During our dinner we witnessed a low caste 'untouchable' man with a cart which was obviously his only means of making money for his family, be hit by a car.

The cart was instantly destroyed and the man lay motionless in a pool of blood in the road. I watched with horror as people noticed and did nothing. Without thinking I ran to the man and sat on the road holding his hand shouting at the crowd that was slowly gathering to call an ambulance. I was horror struck that no one was doing anything and that the life of this man meant nothing to anyone except for me. At this point an Indian man stepped forward and shouted back at me, explaining that in Delhi if you helped someone who was injured and took them to hospital, you became responsible for their medical care and bills.

I had no idea this was the case and had jumped immediately into a judgement space based on my assumption of the caste divide and in this moment, I saw a real-life example of how leadership and infrastructure was actively increasing the poverty gap. My friends and I decided to take financial responsibility for his care and a new cart and ensured that he got to hospital but were left reeling by a system that so obviously punished people that helped those in need.

The following day, we had been asked to speak at a university about leadership and inspire the students with stories of our journey on the tour. What we didn't realise was that the audience also had plenty of the mainstream press attending because the tour was being supported by Prince Philip and Princess Anne. We decided to share the story of what we had witnessed the day before and also our recommendations for a change in policy around medical responsibility for those that couldn't afford care.

We were interviewed afterwards and the story was published. A few months later we were informed by the Confederation of Indian Industry (the tour sponsors) that as a direct result of speaking about the accident and our recommendations, the law had actually been changed in Delhi.

We will never truly know the exact impact of this leadership action or how many lives it has helped to save but it is a great example of how courageously standing up for what you believe in can actually create the very change you are looking for. It is about developing the mindset that every single person has the ability to affect change if they believe that they can.

Our beliefs are also incredibly powerful in the context of strategic leadership action and business success. Over the years I have been asked to work with many organisations on transformation or culture change when they are under performing or facing competitive disadvantage.

Most consultative processes would look at the performance, capacity and capability of specific teams and recommend change or new processes for delivery. This can be a useful short-term coping mechanism but is actually addressing a symptom rather than the root cause of the issue.

The RoundTable philosophy is to look at the leadership in the organisation and discover if there are personal and business limiting beliefs which are filtering down into the culture and consequently the leadership action being delivered. We will start at the top of the company and find out what beliefs the leader has. For example, if they are in the mindset that you have to make mistakes to learn or fail to succeed, this will create a very specific culture and propensity to act in a certain way.

We have worked with leaders whose mentors taught them that you have to get to a place of losing almost everything before you can ultimately succeed. Imagine the subconscious belief system this will create. By helping leaders to identify and release from their fears and self-limiting beliefs we can impact the culture immediately because if they change, the whole organisational eco-system has to change.

Ultimately what we are looking to create is a fear-less culture where anyone at any level can authentically and without judgement of self or others, step into leadership action that effortlessly delivers organisational objectives and exceeds expectations.

True leadership is a special kind of action and stepping courageously into that makes you a special kind of person.

Homework:

The next time you are in a situation either at work or home and you notice that something needs to happen (i.e. a leadership vacuum has been created) practice stepping into it rather than waiting for someone else to. Notice how this feels. What, if anything, comes up for you? How do the people affected by your action respond? Ask for feedback.

Also, think of something that you are passionate about changing in the world. Spend time creating ideas for what you can do to galvanise leadership action towards this. Rather than spending time thinking about and giving energy to the things that we don't want to see in this world, use that energy thinking about what you can do to change it and how you can inspire others to do the same.

Notice what is different, not what is the same.

Authenticity

Being 'authentic' has fast become one of the most aspirational states of being in the leadership and self-help worlds but what does it actually mean? The dictionary definition is 'not false or copied; genuine' which seems simple enough to interpret into everyday life as 'just being yourself' but is it really that easy?

For me being authentic is a state of flow and selfishness. Meaning, that you are authentically making decisions based on what you want rather than what anyone else wants. You may take the desires and needs of others into consideration but ultimately you listen to your body and environment and choose based on what your intuition is telling you. Most people find the thought of being selfish uncomfortable which is an understandable societal conditioned response. Especially for anyone primarily existing in feminine energy–Yin.

Being selfish is seen to be negative and thoughtless, but if you are not making the decisions that you want to make for yourself then you are not truly being authentic. You are adapting, copying, compromising and therefore not being genuine.

This was one of the most difficult learnings for me to truly live as I immersed myself in these philosophies. I found it hard to prioritise my needs let alone put my desires, thoughts and feelings first. It felt cold and masculine.

In fact, my battle with being authentic started when I was at school. I went to quite a rough public secondary school where it was not seen as cool to be academic or interested in learning. I loved learning and I still do. I found both the academic and athletic side of school exciting, interesting and easy and because of that I didn't fit in. This eventually led to me being emotionally and physically bullied by my peers for about four years.

It was a bitter sweet time for me. On the one hand my teachers loved me, I was pretty much a straight-A student and gobbled up work. I loved extra curricula clubs and was captain of the rounders, netball and hockey teams as well as competing in the pentathlon for the athletics club. It was all so easy and effortless for me and I was constantly hungry for more knowledge and to move onto the next thing.

On the other hand, there was a popular gang of girls who felt that I was a show-off and too clever for my own good resulting in them deciding that it was their job to knock me off my pedestal. This combined with the fact that I was an extremely sensitive 'feeling' girl, ensured that I was constantly conflicted about being my authentic self on a day to day basis.

Some days I loved who I was and celebrated my brain and talents, other days I hated myself and 'dumbed down' who I was at school. The more inauthentic I was, the less I was bullied. Being the first one to put my hand up all the time definitely didn't make me any friends. Failing in a test did. Being inauthentic made me more real and accessible. People wanted me to be less than I was and I think this is indicative of the society that we have created. We are attracted to people's idiosyncrasies – they are endearing to us.

It was only when the bullies turned on my sister that I was able to truly step into my authentic self and stand up for us both and what I believed in. What is interesting about this is that I couldn't do it just for myself, I couldn't find the strength and confidence until it became about someone else which again is a very feminine quality. I became a lioness when my sister was threatened.

Subsequently I started to go to kickboxing classes and stepped firmly out of 'victim mode'. What I realise now is that bullies can't bully everyone, they can only bully you if you are in the inauthentic place of doubting who you are and what you do. They play the perfect role in reflecting back to you your insecurities and self-limiting beliefs. As soon as I stepped confidently into my authentic self, the bullying stopped.

Another realisation I have made is that I needed to be bullied. I attracted in the very thing that would not only develop my confidence in being myself but the talent I have for reading people, environments and energies came from that time as I needed to know when to run. That skill set is what has led to me doing the work I do today and because of this I am able to intuitively sense insights about people which enables me to help them unlock potential and clear from limiting beliefs.

Also, there have been two times in my life when my kickboxing skills have seen me out of very tricky and dangerous situations. I don't believe in violence being the answer to anything but knowing some self-defence, especially as a woman has been useful.

This whole story goes back to the RoundTable philosophy of everything happens for a reason / to learn from. I was being bullied because I wasn't able to be truly authentic and confident about my abilities. Because of this I invited in an experience to show me how I felt about myself. This ultimately empowered me to change and once I did, everyone else in my eco-system had to change.

In addition to this, I went through a process where my teachers and friends were telling me to 'toughen up' and I had to choose either to create defensive 'coping mechanisms' or stay authentically open and remain sensitive. Thank fully at such a young age, I decided on the latter. To remain an open person wearing my heart on my sleeve, knowing that at times this might hurt but also enabling me to develop my intuition and sensing of others.

Although it was traumatic at the time, with the benefit of time and awareness I am now extremely grateful for the experience I had at school. It made me a much more authentic person and now I never try to fit in or be anyone other than who I am. Regardless of who I am with or what I am doing. Absolutely everyone gets the same version of me and this has also served me.

I mentioned before about the female leadership programme that I designed and delivered for the first time in a temple in Tokyo but what I didn't mention was that this programme led me to meet and ultimately work directly with the First Lady of Japan, Mrs Akie Abe.

This is an important story as it relates to authenticity and how we energetically feel each other. The programme I had co-designed with my team was called Flourish and had been created in response to the Prime Minister of Japan, Shinzō Abe focusing on bringing more women into leadership roles. I had become concerned that without a culture change towards feminine leadership in organisations we would be setting women up to fail.

I believe it was because we created Flourish as a culture change movement rather than a female leadership programme, we caught the attention of Mrs Abe and we arranged to meet over tea which turned out to be a pivotal moment in my career.

During that meeting I passionately and with complete authenticity told Mrs Abe about who I was, what I stood for and my desire to create real change in the world through education and the development of feminine leadership. It is my belief that Mrs Abe who is an astute judge of character sensed and connected to my authenticity and emotionally offered her support to the work I was doing globally. I didn't pretend to be anyone else or try and be what I thought she might want me to be. I was 100% myself and I respectfully treated her like a human being passionate about empowerment and change.

There is so much more to this story, including the fact that Mrs Abe and I went on to create the 'En Committee' – a group of influential women from around the world focused on feminine leadership and that our meeting was the catalyst for me starting RoundTable with my co-founders but for now I just want to reiterate the importance of my authenticity in our ability to energetically connect.

Being truly authentic can be confronting and disarming. Confronting for you and anyone that is being inauthentic and disarming because it is so honest.

So how do we know if we are being authentic and if not, how do we start on the journey towards this? The first question you have to ask yourself is 'are you making that decision or choice for you or for someone else?' and then 'are you acting in flow or consciously trying to be something that you think you should be?'. Being inauthentic can be exhausting. Constantly trying to please other people and make them happy depletes your energy as you are working against your natural state of effortless flow.

Being selfish, or prioritising yourself is healthy. Not necessarily at the detriment of others but with the intention to ensure that you are happy and healthy. The more time and energy you give to yourself, rejuvenation and growth, the more abundance you have to give to everyone else.

If you combine this state of being with genuinely taking 100% responsibility for everything you are creating and learn from it, you will find it easier and quicker to release from your subconscious patterns and beliefs so that you can unlock your potential and evolve to becoming the best version of yourself.

Taking time for you to understand and appreciate who you are is the first step towards being authentic. Listening to what your body and environment is telling you as you interact with others and make decisions and choices in the next step. You know when you are doing something that you don't want to do. What is beautiful about becoming more authentic is that you give permission to everyone in your eco-system to do the same.

Homework:

As you are making choices and decisions over the coming days listen to your body. Do you get tired, feel emotional, angry or frustrated? If you do then you know that you are not being authentic. Watch your interactions with other people, are you adapting your personality and contributions based on what you think they want to see?

Prioritise yourself, spend time each week doing things that you love that increase your energy and rejuvenate you. Notice how this abundance enables you to give more (quality) attention and time to others in your eco-system. Notice what is different, not what is the same.

Relationships – Not Labels

Our ability to be truly authentic is also affected by our attachment to the labels that we have in our lives. What I mean by this is the 'noun labels' we have. The labels that define a specific relationship with another human being such as being a daughter or a son not 'adjective labels' like funny, happy or silly.

When we are delivering a session on labels either during Shine or our other programmes, we ask the participants to write their name in the middle of a page and then identify as many different labels they have as possible. Here are some of mine so that you get the picture.

I am a daughter, sister, aunt, cousin, granddaughter, niece, friend, best friend, employer, professional, supplier, facilitator, neighbour, partner, co-founder, girlfriend, student, teacher…the list goes on. I guarantee that if you are doing this activity right now, there will be at least ten labels that you haven't thought of. The point is that we have a lot.

Now, there is nothing wrong with having labels – they are useful. It is helpful for people in my eco-system to understand who my sister is or if I have a 'best friend'. As humans, we crave belonging to specific communities and labels can fulfil our need for this.

It is not having labels that effects our ability to be authentic. It is our attachment to the expectations they create. Think about that for a moment.

Every single label we have has three sets of expectations. For the purposes of this book I am going to use the label daughter. Regardless of whether we still have parents in this world or what our relationship with them is, at some point every human being has been a son or daughter.

Being a daughter comes with the expectation of what I think is a good and bad daughter, what I think my parents think is a good and bad daughter and what they actually think is a good and bad daughter. If I am constantly trying to be a good version of all three of these sets of expectations, how often am I making decisions that are truly authentic to me?

Combine this with my parent's expectations around what is a good and bad parent and you can be certain that we are all constantly doing things that we don't want to do based on our attachment to be the 'good' version of our labels. Now times that by all of the labels you have in your life and it is no wonder that we find being authentic difficult.

Let me bring this to life for you. Let's say I leave home for the first time to go to university and my mum is really worried and sad so she makes me promise that I will come every Sunday so she can feed me, make sure I have clean clothes and some money. This is what she believes she should do as a 'good mother' and I agree as I feel guilty that she is worrying and I want to be a 'good daughter'.

20 years later when I am still going home every Sunday, are we both being authentic? Probably not but our attachment to what is a good daughter and mother is holding us both in an energetic hug, a subconscious pattern that is so powerful in its longevity that no-one wants to break it for fear of upsetting the other. This is what I mean by being attached to the expectation.

Having expectations of the people in your life is OK. It allows them to understand what you feel that you need and want but not being attached to them liberates your eco-system to be authentic and to redefine expectations based on what you both actually want. In the example of the Sunday visits between mother and daughter – if there was no attachment, either could cancel, reschedule or change the expectation at any time without fear of being a bad mother or daughter.

We are constantly evolving and changing and being in this non-attached mindset allows us to redefine our relationships with others in alignment with our development, which in turn empowers us and those in our eco-system to be authentically themselves all of the time.

Let me give you another example because not only are we attached to the expectations of ourselves in these labels but we also treat other people differently based on the attachment to what their labels mean to us.

Let's say that I have a friend and when he gets drunk, he dances on the table which we all think is hilarious. In fact, it is his free spirited, fun loving nature that makes me want to have him as a best friend but once he becomes my best friend, I'm not so sure if I want him dancing on the table. As his best friend I think I should be more responsible for him, that I should make sure he gets home OK at the end of the night. Then he becomes my boyfriend and my expectation of a boyfriend is that he will look after me and not get drunk and dance on the table so I ask him not to. Then he proposes and becomes my fiancé which means I believe his behaviour reflects badly on me when he gets drunk so I tell him how I feel. Then he becomes my husband and a good husband doesn't get drunk and dance on the table, right? So, I tell him he is not allowed to. Then he becomes the father of my child and needs to be a good role model so I tell him if he gets drunk and dances on the table, I will leave him.

Six different labels, 18 attachments to being the 'good' variation of these labels and then this can happen within two years. The very thing that attached me to that person in the first place becomes the thing that I am desperate to change and try and force him to change because of the attachment to my expectations around these labels.

How can either of us be authentic in this paradigm? I am forcing myself to take on the role of oppressor and dictator, and I am also trying to make another person change to fit my expectations.

One thing I have learned for certain in this life is that we can't change anyone except for ourselves. We can influence change in others for a period of time but it is unsustainable and ultimately, they will revert back to being who they really are or will become an exaggerated version of that in rebellion.

So, in this case, if my expectations are that my boy-friend/fiancé/husband/father of my children shouldn't be getting drunk and dancing on the table then rather being attached to this I need to look at changing myself. Not necessarily meaning that my expectations need to change but I can choose whether to be there or not and also how to react if I am there. For example, if I stop being there without any reprimand or ultimatum to my partner, essentially freeing him up to do whatever he wants, maybe this change in me will stimulate him to want to change himself. Maybe he will miss my company, maybe not. The point is that I will be freeing him up to be authentic and I don't take on the responsibility to change him.

A real-life version of this was with my last partner who was in an introverted phase due to writing his book and also not wanting to socialise or drink too much. My expectation at first was that we should do everything together and so I constantly made plans for us and was either disappointed when he declined them or I acted unauthentically and cancelled them, despite wanting to go, so that we could spend time together.

After a while of me really living these philosophies I realised that I was attached to the label of what a good 'boyfriend' was which was holding us both in that energetic hug and not allowing us to make authentic decisions for ourselves.

Once I realised this, I started to make plans for myself and let him know what I was going to do with an open invite for him to join me. This was hugely liberating for both of us as I didn't feel like a 'bad' girlfriend for doing what I wanted on the weekends while he wrote and he didn't feel pressured to come with me. The most interesting outcome of which was that he started wanting to come with me and actively making plans for us too.

There is a saying that you can lead a horse to water but you can't make him drink and I believe that this is true for having healthy relationships rather than being attached to labels. You can tell the people you have relationships with what you want from them but you then need to allow them to authentically decide what they want within those expectations.

Ultimately if your expectations are so fundamentally different that you can't be authentic and stay together, maybe it is time for the label to change or for you to look beyond the label and understand that we are all unique, individual human beings with our own stuff going on and our own subconscious patterns and expectations.

On that note, we can also get blindsided by labels and forget to treat each other as humans. One of the things I decided to do when I realised the power of non-attachment to labels was spend time with my parents finding out who they were before I existed, what their hopes, dreams and fears are and how I could support them on their journey in life.

It is worth remembering that we are all just people trying to make our way in this crazy beautiful world and never has this been more powerful to me than when I lost my father in a tragic accident recently. Although he and my mother split up when I was only four and he effectively left us, through these philosophies I have never held him in the pattern of being a bad father. Instead I got to know him as a person and he became one of my best friends in the world.

Every time I met him, I was able to do so for the first time and not hold him in any patterns of behaviour or expectations. I will always be grateful for this as our time together was beautiful, full of fun and nourishing for both of us.

Another powerful example of how non-attachment to labels can serve you is in the workplace. A few years ago, I ran a Shine programme for 19 women from a company in Iran and when we got onto the subject of labels, they couldn't wait to tell me about this 'bad boss' they all had. It was their belief that because they were in collective agreement about this – they all thought he was bad, that their attachment to expectations were OK.

So, I asked them about the boss they had before, the 'good boss'. They enthusiastically told me about how personable he was and how he went out of his way to get to know them and spend time with them and that every Friday afternoon they had social/fun time which they loved and had not been continued with the new boss who came to work, walked passed them all into his office and then shut the door for the day.

When I asked them why the old boss had left, they told me that the company had been underperforming and that he had been let go based on this. I asked how the business was doing now and they told me that performance and sales were up and that everything was looking good.

At this point I helped them to realise that what they were labelling and being attached to in terms of a 'good boss' may have eventually meant that they no longer had jobs and the new 'bad boss' was at the very least ensuring their job security.

This led to some contemplation and eventually went back to the attachment that he still wasn't a good boss as he didn't seem care about them. This enabled me to remind them that the new boss was a human being and that he would be able to energetically feel that 19 women in the office didn't like him which I suspect would cause anyone to retreat to the safety of an office behind a closed door to do the work required to save the company.

I also asked if any of them had introduced themselves to the new boss or asked how he was and what he might need? Had anyone offered to show him around and introduce him to the team? The answer was no because in their attachment of a 'good boss' they saw that as his job, not theirs.

Once they realised that he was a human being with a gnarly, high pressured job on his hands that potentially affected them all, they realised that they needed to change and release him from the energetic hug. Meaning one of them knocked on his door, asked him how he was doing and ultimately took it upon herself to introduce him to everyone for which he was not only relieved but immensely grateful and they realised that actually he was a lovely person under a lot of stress and pressure.

Being attached to labels can lead to disappointment for you and pressure/stress for the other person. Liberation from attachment means that you can both authentically bring your-selves to the relationship and make choices from a genuine place.

Homework:

Spend time writing down all of the labels you have in your life. Think about each person relevant to the relationship and whether you are treating them according to your expectation around the label or as a unique, individual human being. Think about your role in the relationship. Are you being authentic and true to yourself? What would you change and do differently if you could? Spend time getting to know who the people in your ecosystem really are outside of the labels. What does this change for you and for them?

Notice what is different, not what is the same.

Follow Your Bliss

"Follow your bliss. If you do follow your bliss, you put yourself on a kind of track that has been there all the while waiting for you, and the life you ought to be living is the one you are living. When you can see that, you begin to meet people who are in the field of your bliss, and they open the doors to you. I say, follow your bliss and don't be afraid, and doors will open where you didn't know they were going to be. If you follow your bliss, doors will open for you that wouldn't have opened for anyone else."

This is one of my favourite quotes by Joseph Campbell and I often simplify it by saying 'find what you love doing and are passionate about and do more of it'. That is my definition of bliss. Waking up every day and regardless of what happens, knowing that I am pursuing the things that I love doing that make a difference and spending time with the people that I love and enjoy while doing them.

The world is full of people who are unhappy in their jobs and their relationships who can't even imagine a life that is different. People who spend their days looking forward to the weekend and dreading Mondays. Creating eco-systems and environments that are screaming at them to make a change until eventually the decision is made for them. They are so fearful of taking a step into the unknown that it often takes a serious illness or dramatic catalyst for them to take notice and make the change.

Do you think that the person who is made redundant, demoted or sacked really loves their job and has been working to their full potential with enthusiasm and bliss?

Most people know someone in their life who has been through something 'traumatic' or 'life threatening' forcing them to rethink everything and choose a different path and the majority of them when looking back say 'I am so glad that it happened because now I love my life and am doing what I always wanted to do'.

Our conscious mind which is what we know we know, is constantly making decisions based on our subconscious fears, patterns and beliefs. So, for example if we have been brought up to believe that we should be earning a certain amount of money by a specific age or own a house / be married / have children etc., this will inform the decisions that we make.

We may stay in a job that we don't really enjoy and convince ourselves that we are 'lucky' and 'happy' because everyone else sees us as successful and congratulates us on doing so well. The thought of stepping away from a well-paid, secure job, especially when you have a family and bills to pay can be unimaginable or seem impossible but ultimately if we are subconsciously hiding the truth from ourselves and not listening to our intuition – we will eventually create a catalyst for change.

Let me tell you a story to bring this to life. Let's say that I work for a famous advertising agency in London and I am one of the most senior women in the company. I work and travel all the time but I earn great money and have fantastic perks. My friends are envious of how well I am doing. Then I get offered an opportunity to go to New York and open our first office there. I tell myself that this is real testament to how well I am doing. I will have even more money and be managing a large team of creatives. I am excited.

Before I can move, I have a final interview for my visa that I can't miss. The morning of the interview I wake up and realise that my alarm hasn't gone off. I am angry at myself as I always set my alarm and I can't believe that on such an important day I forgot. I rush to get dressed, run down stairs to make breakfast and while printing off my forms I forget my toast and it burns so I have to make some more. Now I'm really running late so I put my coffee in a thermos without the lid because it has mysteriously gone missing and as I am running out of the door I trip and spill the coffee all over myself. Scalding my chest and ruining my outfit.

Meaning I have to go back upstairs and change. At this point I am getting seriously stressed and am worried about missing the interview so as I leave my house, I am looking at my phone to find the number to call and let them know I am running late. While looking at the phone I step out into the road, get hit by a car and break my leg in three places.

Now there is no way that I can make the interview and also no way I will still be offered to job as they need someone to travel to New York ASAP and I will be in hospital for weeks.

I am devastated and my conscious mind is full of blame for myself, the alarm clock, the toaster, who ever lost the coffee cup lid and the driver of the car. I am seeing the whole experience as the worst thing that has ever happened to me and I am angry. The angrier I get, the more pain I am in and the worse my situation seems.

Eventually, after some days I start to calm down and 'accept' the situation. It takes a lot of energy to be angry and I realise there is nothing I can do. As I stop feeding the anger/ blame story, the pain in my leg lessens and I start to heal faster. This makes me feel better. So, I ask myself the question, why have I created this and I realise that I now have a lot of paid for time on my hands.

Time to read all of the leadership and personal development books I have been buying and stockpiling for 'when I have time' (which was never). Time to watch all of the documentaries I have been saving on Netflix and YouTube. As I do, a sense of calm overcomes me for the first time in years. I am enjoying this time to learn and enjoying not being under such high-level pressure all the time.

So, I start to ask myself the questions – do I really love being in advertising? Does it fulfil me and give me a sense of purpose over and above making me 'feel' successful? Is this really what I want to do for the rest of my life and more importantly do I want to live in New York? I allow myself the time to really listen to myself, to explore the idea of doing something different and as I do, I start to feel excited.

I realise that I don't even like advertising and that the people I work with are not friends they are colleagues, people that I am actively competing with in a masculine way on a day to day basis.

I decided that I am going to quit and focus my attention on something that gives me purpose. That fulfils my deep longing to contribute in a meaningful way to society and as I make this decision creative ideas for what I want to do come bubbling into my conscious, they fill my dreams and my thoughts and as I allow this excitement to build, my leg is healing even faster. I am feeling rejuvenated from years of pressure and stress that I didn't even know had been building up.

I decide to quit my coffee and toast diet and to experiment with cooking and decide to start eating only plant-based foods. My leg heals faster and the doctors can't believe it. So much so that I can start my physiotherapy early and when I meet my therapist, I am not surprised to find that he is gorgeous, a vegetarian and wants to set up his own business helping people. We fall in love, set up a business together and get married.

Suddenly the most awful thing that ever happened to me becomes the best thing. It is the start of our story and the beginning of me moving into a flow state towards my bliss. With the benefit of hindsight, I never wanted to move away and I didn't love my job. It took an extreme catalyst, a shout, for me to realise that my bliss was a different path and without this catalyst I wouldn't have met my partner or started a business that I love.

You see how it works? I had whispers before the shout. The alarm clock not going off when I 'always' set it was a whisper. The burned toast and spilt coffee were louder whispers which I didn't listen to so I had to create a shout to get my attention.

Now this isn't a true story for me but I know so many people who have had to create a shout in their lives to help them overcome the fear of change and that shout was exactly what needed to happen for them.

Living these philosophies and setting an intention towards following my bliss means that I am constantly seeking to listen to the whispers. If I am late for something, miss my plane, get sick or have someone change plans on me – I ask myself the question why I have created it and what it is enabling me to do or preventing me from doing.

I don't believe that there is such a thing as self-sabotage, I think our subconscious is constantly creating experiences to show us what we really want in our lives and it is up to us to listen.

I know people who have recovered from cancer and as a result completely changed their lifestyle and diet and also allowed themselves to do what they love doing without any guilt.

I know people whose partners have 'cheated' on them and come to the realisation that they no longer wanted to be in the relationship but were fearful of being the 'bad' person by leaving. They realised that they energetically pushed their partner away so that they would fulfil their role perfectly and create a situation where they could both be free of the relationship.

As humans we are extremely good at hiding how we really feel from ourselves and not listening to what our bodies and environments are telling us. This is why the check in is so important and why I check in with myself every day.

Another thing that prevents many people from following their bliss is the fear that if you do what you love doing you won't be able to make money from it and that simply isn't true.

Absolutely everything can be monetised, you just have to think creatively about how to proactively create a demand. I have worked with hundreds of people who didn't believe that they could get paid well or at all for what they love doing who are now blissfully doing that thing on a day to day basis.

I have a friend who loves food, travel and meeting new exciting people who is now paid to review travel destinations, hotels and restaurants. She put that intention out there and as soon as she did, she started attracting in those opportunities. A bit like my desire to speak and share my message as mentioned in a previous chapter and suddenly I was getting requests to deliver Ted X's and MC global summits and forums.

When you are in fear-less flow you can effortlessly attract in exactly what you need to continue in that space. It is your fears and limiting beliefs that create the glass ceilings and block your ability to create.

In the short term if you can identify what you love doing and are passionate about and do more of it while still continuing with your current reality, you will start attracting opportunities and people that will assist on your journey into following your bliss and being in your authentic flow.

Homework:

We spend a lot of time thinking about what we don't like and the things that we don't want in our lives but most people don't spend any time thinking about what they do want. In fact, many people I have worked with don't even know what they want or what they love doing.

Take a piece of paper and divide it into four squares. Close your eyes, take a deep breath, connect to the body and when you open your eyes write the word 'Love' in one of the squares. Give yourself three to five minutes to write all of the things that come into your mind when you think about love. Then repeat the process for 'Work' 'Health' and 'Dreams'.

Try not the think too hard – you are seeking a free flow of consciousness that enables your subconscious to speak to you.

Once you have finished share your paper and thinking with someone in your eco-system. Ask them to help you identify what your dream is and what you would love to do. The following chapters will help you to formulate a plan to move towards this.

Notice what is different, not what is the same.

Finding Balance
Masculine and Feminine
Energies

I am really excited about writing this chapter as the exploration of masculine and feminine leadership energies has fascinated me for years. It has been the driving force for me starting RoundTable Global with my co-founders and the inspiration for everything to do with Shine.

The thing that I find most exciting about the concepts of masculine and feminine is that without social stereotyping, they are genderless, powerful energies that all of us require in balance to unlock our full potential and thrive.

There is a global misconception that women own the feminine and men own masculine and it is this that creates the divisiveness between genders. We are taught from the moment we can fully understand that men and women are different and should act accordingly. We are even punished by our parents, educators and peers for 'acting out'.

The truth is that masculine and feminine are like Yin and Yang and each of us, regardless of gender, can tap into a unique balance of them both that is completely individual. Like a finger print. Your balance of masculine and feminine when embraced authentically will empower you to be the best version of yourself, it will enable you to prioritise and take care of yourself so that you have abundance for everyone else in your eco-system.

Masculine energy is focused on self. Self-preservation, protection, health, growth, personal development, success, ensuring you have everything you need, prioritising you over everything else and most important of all, making sure that you are always being authentically you. This is why men find it easier in our current reality construct to be 'selfish' and to be bold about what they are great at.

Feminine energy is focused on other. Community, collaboration, effective communication, creativity, making sure that everyone in the eco-system is OK, well-fed, has everything they need and well. Checking in with everyone, sharing time, resources, thoughts and feelings. The feminine seeks to prioritise everyone else without a thought to self which is why having a balance of masculine is so important. Being mostly in the feminine, often leads to burn out, demotivation and a sense of despondency. You spend so much time giving to and taking care of everyone else that you run out of energy for you.

The good news is that finding your balance within the energies is effortless once you step into being completely authentically you. The social stereotyping, we have collectively created that attributes masculine and feminine energies to genders is a subconscious pattern that can be changed once your belief system changes.

There is so much in the media today about how women are disempowered and repressed which has led to a huge global focus on increasing the number of female leaders in policy and business decision-making. I believe that this is an important priority because we need more feminine leadership energy in the world (and women currently are more comfortable in that space) but that we also need to look at changing how we educate our young.

What I mean by this is that women have been fighting for equality as 'feminists' for years at the same time as propagating the masculine and feminine energy divide as carriers of the culture. At the moment it is mostly women who stay at home and bring up the children.

It is women who are teaching the next generation about what it means to be a girl or a boy.

I have worked with the most senior women in some of the biggest organisations in the world, key speakers at 'Lean In' and other empowerment summits and conferences who have no idea until they participate in Shine that they are actually propagating the gender divide at home. They are subconsciously teaching their daughters that they should be feminine and their sons to be masculine.

It is exciting for me to be with these women when the penny drops and they realise that they have been talking about a 'glass ceiling' that we as women are helping to create. One of the women I worked with a few years ago was astounded when she realised that she had been stopping her daughter from playing soccer as it wasn't feminine. A few months after Shine she let me know that her daughter was so good, she was playing on the boys' team at a national level and had never been as happy.

I have so many stories like this. Stories of sons that don't have to tidy their own bedrooms, aren't expected to share or contribute to household chores, are allowed to do what they want when they want and also expected to not cry, show vulnerability, never be like a girl and should be the man of the house. They are taught to be the providers, the earners, the strong ones and to compete to win at all times.

I have stories of daughters that are expected to be kind hearted, generous and giving. They must contribute, tidy, always be honest, never answer back and always put friends and family first. They are taught to not be assertive, ambitious or to show any aggression, ever. They are told they will never find a husband if they are seen as too strong, bossy or demanding.

These sons then become men in their masculine, always striving for survival and success, unable to demonstrate or effectively communicate how they feel. These daughters become women in their feminine disempowered and repressed, second guessing their decisions and never prioritising themselves.

This is why I am so fascinated and excited by the concept of each of us finding our balance. Our ability to step authentically and healthily into both the prioritisation of self at the same time as the consideration of others. Imagine being able to reach your full potential as a human and having the desire to share your skills and talents so that everyone in your eco-system can do the same?

This is the journey that I am fully immersed in personally and Shine is the springboard for anyone else wishing to find their personal balance. It is time for us to stop focusing on just women's leadership and female empowerment and to include a global culture change towards finding balance in the masculine and feminine.

We need to create leadership teams that empower every single person to tap into both masculine and feminine energies, organisations that enable their people to authentically bring their whole-selves to work by providing personal development and sustainable mindset change towards this goal.

Decisions made from a place of supportive competition, creativity and collaboration will thrust organisations effortlessly into a place of thriving rather than surviving. Organisations that are focusing on the triple bottom line reporting of People, Planet and Profit are already outperforming those that aren't. Traditional masculine, patriarchal organisations that are just focused on success and survival (profit) are now struggling to attract and retain both talent and long-term customers.

There is a new paradigm of organisations like RoundTable, social enterprises or responsible businesses that are tapping into the feminine leadership energies of people (stakeholders, talent, community and consumers) and planet (environmental rejuvenation) as a unique differentiator and a way of capturing the imagination of potential partners and customers.

It is our Three Global Goals of Educational Innovation, Empowering Everyone and Environmental Rejuvenation that connects with our clients and contributors enabling us to scale our delivery to over 20 countries in just four years. People that meet us from all over the world are inspired by our story of focusing on making a real difference in the world at the same time as generating our own revenue to do it.

We have effortlessly created real balance in our masculine and feminine leadership energies in RoundTable meaning that to date we have been able to fund all of our philanthropic

(People, Planet) initiatives with the revenue (Profits) from the commercial side of our business. A completely self-sustaining enterprise which has allowed us to be agile in our desire to scale and discerning in our choice of partners and clients.

In fact, when we created Round-Table we consciously agreed to not have a business strategy which we felt might limit our potential and create fear or stress and instead to be in energetic flow with delivering our Three Global Goals from a place of supportive competition and collaboration (masculine and feminine balance). Meaning we wanted to do things differently from everyone else, tapping into imagination, creativity and play at the same time as sharing absolutely everything.

This book is a great example of that in action. Everything you are reading here is in our Shine Programme and we are openly sharing our knowledge and philosophies so that other people can challenge them, build on the concepts and theories and encourage us to continuously evolve and innovate our thinking and methodologies.

Being in a place of balance means being in a fear-less place. A mindset and way of being that is guided by authentic intuition and the understanding that we are all one. If we each look after ourselves in a way that is healthy and considerate, we will impact the greater eco-system with creativity and abundance.

Our socially conditioned misconceptions around masculine and feminine have also impacted our ability to have healthy intimate and sexual relationships with one another as we attribute certain expectations and behaviours to the gender rather than the individual. If a woman makes it clear that she would like to have sex she can be seen as 'forward' (negative) where as men in the same position can be seen as 'initiating' (positive). Men who have lots of sexual partners are often portrayed as 'players' and 'charmers' (mostly positive) where are women are seen as 'promiscuous' (negative).

This means that often both partners are unable to be completely sexually authentic because of the attachment to how they should behave based on being masculine or feminine. I am sure most men don't always want to initiate or have sex and that there are lots of women who would like to be much more demanding in and out of the bedroom without fear of being judged.

The sheer volume of self-help books orientated towards cementing the belief systems that men and women are different is astounding and certainly contributes to our currently inability to see each other as unique, individual human beings rather than specific genders.

Having said this, I do think that there is a growing awareness and consciousness around masculine and feminine balance and unique identity that is showing up as gender confusion and in the constant creation of new 'gender labels' because the masculine male and feminine female are not truly authentic for anyone. Perhaps if we could all find our balance, we would not need to seek labels and instead embrace our unique individuality and allow ourselves to love and be loved unconditionally.

There is so much I could share regarding my explorations of masculine and feminine, the impact they have had on cultures and ultimately on how we have arrived at our current global reality but that would take a whole book rather than a chapter. Instead I am going to share with you a philosophy around this concept that I haven't even fully thought out yet – I think it is a powerful theory to ponder and build on and may help us to understand why we have created the masculine and feminine divide.

Regardless of your belief system or religion, let's say that in most creation stories there is a divine feminine and a divining masculine. The feminine is the ability to create life (other) and the masculine is the ability to survive and therefore if need be, to take life (self). This is the balance of Yin and Yang. Life and death.

There is no doubting the fact that women have evolved to be able to create life, of course this cannot be achieved without the male sperm but ultimately it is the woman who carries and builds the life within her body. Her energy, blood and cells create the human that is eventually born. It is an inherent divine power that most women have. Because of this gift, women have to be in the feminine 'other' to ensure the survival and health of the child.

As a contrast, men cannot currently conceive or carry children. Other than providing seed for conception they do not have to continue to contribute to the life of the child. I often wonder how it feels to be a man without that divine power of carrying life. I don't have children myself so I can't profess to know what it is actually like to give birth but at least I have had the choice.

So, because the ultimate divine feminine of life giving has fallen to the female, does that mean that a subconscious divine masculine of life taking or ruling through fear of death has through history fallen to men?

It is a heady but thought-provoking theory. 95% of the time that we have been on this planet we have been at war. The quest for power and dominance has been the biggest killer of human kind and throughout history the leadership of this is shown as being masculine patriarchal societies led predominantly by men.

Do men feel that they have to step into and own this divine power because we are all out of balance and they do not appreciate the significance of their role in the divinity of life itself? Do women cower away from standing up for themselves and their survival because of their subconsciously inherent belief that they are alive to create and nurture life rather than to control what happens with it?

When you think about it, it is obvious that our male/female divide stems from our biological differences and of course this creates hormonal and chemical reactions in our bodies that can affect our behaviour but it is this deeper, more profound subconscious belief system that I propose impacts how we as individuals show up in the world.

Finding our own unique balance of masculine and feminine will empower us to authentically and effortlessly thrive and contribute to the global community and ecosystem.

Homework:

Spend some time thinking about the beliefs you have around men and women. How are they different? What have you been taught? How do you feel that your gender has affected your ability to be authentic? What are you doing that you don't want to do and what would you like to do if you weren't fearful of being judged?

Have a look at the people in your eco-system – are you projecting your beliefs or subconscious gender bias onto them? Do you have children? What are you teaching them about the feminine and masculine?

Notice what is different, not what is the same.

The Power of Imagination

I invited a new member of the Round-Table team to join a one-day Shine workshop the other day and was really interested at the immediate sense of fear she demonstrated at the thought of having to connect, share and disclose personal thoughts and feelings. When we explored what exactly felt triggering, she described a sense of heaviness that she attributed to 'therapy' and 'self-help' which in her mind were part of all empowerment programmes and workshops.

For her the thought of having to dig deep into her psyche and bring up memories of trauma and personal discomfort in front of a group of relative strangers was frightening and upsetting and this is what she thought the objective of the workshop was.

One of the many things that I love about the design and delivery of Shine is that we have focused on developing methodologies and philosophies that do not require participants to re-live the past or to share/disclose anything that they don't feel comfortable with. We have purposefully made our programmes as creative and playful as possible so that everyone has fun at the same time as having profound realisations and personal transformations.

Our workshops are about as far from traditional classroom-based training programmes as you can get and most of the time, participants forget that they are actually learning. The experiences that we create are exciting, immersive and experiential with a combined focus on individual and group development.

We start every programme with the Bruce Lee quote *'Take what is useful, discard what is useless and uniquely make it your own'*. We use this to explain to participants that although we are offering new ideas and different ways of thinking that can lead to a huge amount of change, they are just offerings and we are not attached to everyone leaving with the same belief systems and philosophies as us.

We explain that everyone in the room is a unique individual human being with their own experiences and personal belief systems and that we do not expect everything to land for everyone. This frees them up to challenge, ask questions and to focus on what really resonates for them rather than feeling defensive about anything that is triggering.

This is the difference between being in a judgement (masculine) energy and an opinion (feminine) energy. A judgement is saying 'I believe and therefore you should believe...' closing off discussion and creating teacher/student separation and an opinion is 'I believe and I invite you to explore with me...' which is much softer and open. All of our facilitators are taught to deliver our content in this way which in itself is unique in the learning and development world.

I absolutely love the freedom that this gives me as a facilitator to be creative with my delivery. I feel that at the same time as holding the space for the groups I work with I am able to read the room and diverge our discussions based on the questions and challenges I get. I am constantly evolving our content through these experiences as well as developing my intuition and ability to change the course of the programme or workshop based on what the group requires. In those moments I am the student as well as the teacher and it requires dynamic creativity and innovation to engage with everyone and find our way back to the rest of the content in a meaningful way.

It is fun, playful and inclusive. Even when the topics we are exploring are quite challenging.

One of the driving objectives for RoundTable has been the bringing together of the corporate and creative worlds for mutual benefit. Having worked in the learning and development industry for nearly 20 years I have witnessed the regurgitation and adaption of leadership and empowerment programmes where those being forced to participate in them experience learning burn-out and often don't turn up or are only there in body for the duration.

I have personally participated in the most mind numbing, disengaging programmes where I have been talked at and taught in such a way that I've had to drink gallons of coffee to just stay awake.

None of our programmes are like this. We have purposefully sought out talented contributors who are expert creatives in their own fields and worked with them to turn their gorgeous experiences into opportunities for people to learn about themselves. We capture the imagination of our participants and empower them to tap into parts of their minds and bodies that they haven't utilised for a long time.

One of the most powerful and healing ways we do this is through the imagination. As adults, the majority of us think that we are still using our imaginations on a regular basis. We believe we are tapping into this immense store of truly unique thinking and ideas when in actual fact most people have replaced imagination with visualisation. Which is not the same.

When we are picturing the future and thinking about what we believe we want such as setting intentions or dreams, for the most part we are visualising. We are using our conscious minds to build an image and a story for us to work towards and follow. It is structured and based on our patterns and beliefs for what happiness and success looks like for us. This is not using our imaginations as it is what we know that we know.

Our imaginations are gateways into our subconscious minds and allow us to access the information that we don't know we know. They are exciting archives full of everything we have ever experienced, learned, felt, seen, heard and encountered which is too much information for us to have to filter on a regular basis but can be accessed so we can learn more about who we are and what our subconscious beliefs are. To bring this to life, imagine walking down a corridor that has pictures covering the walls on both sides and your immediate attention is on the door at the end of the corridor. If I asked you what you saw as you walked most people would mention the pictures but not feel able to describe any in detail unless they had consciously looked at them. It would seem impossible that you would be able to remember all of them but in theory this is the power of the subconscious. If you were able to access it in a controlled way you would be able to not only remember every single picture but also describe them in detail.

This is why our imaginations are the most powerful tool we have available to us. Like dreaming they provide a safe and often fun and playful place for us to explore how we feel about the things we have learned and experienced. They allow us to mix fantasy with reality and have realisations leading to the release of our self-limiting beliefs and fears without having to share them with anyone else or re-live them ourselves.

Our imaginations are also truly unique and private meaning that we can be really honest with ourselves and authentically explore what is coming up for us emotionally and physically.

Have you ever gone to bed at night with a challenge or issue that you can't find a solution for and when you wake up in the morning it is clear to you what you need to do and you have plenty of ideas? This is your subconscious mind working for you while you sleep and dream and using your imagination is just a lucid version of this.

This happens for me all of the time. If I am struggling to find a creative solution or I feel that my limiting beliefs and fears are stopping me from doing something I need to do, I will either go into my imagination or have a sleep and nine times out of 10 the answer is revealed to me. On the few occasions that it is not, I have a great rest and work on something else for a while until the solution becomes clear.

As far as I can see there is no downside to tapping into the power of your imagination for subconscious healing and unique creativity. Even if it ends up with you having a lovely rejuvenating sleep, it is working without you knowing.

During Shine we take participants through a guided process of remembering how to use imagination specifically for personal realisations, healing and releasing. An example would be where we ask everyone to think about something or someone that makes them feel mad, sad or guilty until they feel it somewhere in their body or can feel the emotion.

We never ask anyone to disclose what they are thinking about which means that they can be absolutely honest to themselves without fear of being judged.

Once they are able to tap into the emotion or physical feeling we talk them through a six to eight minutes imagination journey where we suggest scenarios for them to imagine themselves in (such as 'imagine you are at the top of a mountain – what can you see?') and then provide space for their subconscious to kick in and feed what they imagine. What they see during this journey means something with regard to the 'mad, sad, guilty' thing they had thought of but we don't need to analyse it for them to have realisations and change.

Before we end the imagination journeys we have developed, we take the participants back to the place they imagined at the start and ask them to notice what is different. This is important as if what they are imagining has changed, more often than not something in the subconscious has changed and the person has changed.

After the journey we then ask the participants to try and return to the physical or emotional feeling of bad, sad, guilty and to notice if it is different. For most people the feeling is either more neutral, has completely disappeared or changed in some way. They feel differently about the thing they had been thinking about and often physical ailments associated with the experience or person lessen or can completely disappear.

A great example of this is when I was working with a lady in the Middle East who had been in two minor road accidents and had developed a fear of even being able to get into a car. Anytime she thought about having to go anywhere she would start to display the physical and emotional stress symptoms of anyone experiencing a severe phobia. This had been affecting her ability to travel for the past two years.

During her imagination journey she had the realisation that her phobia had been serving her as she had been asked to travel for work and was worried about leaving her elderly parents at home alone. The travel phobia gave her a guilt free excuse for not working away from home. What was important about this realisation was that she was holding herself in the pattern of being a 'good daughter' and not allowing herself to even consider what she actually thought would be a great personal development and career opportunity for her. She chose to share this realisation with me and I helped her to understand that she was projecting her assumptions on her parents and not giving them an opportunity to let her know their authentic thoughts and feelings on the matter. She was so worried about 'letting them down' that she didn't even include them in the discussion.

That evening she sat and spoke to her parents who were excited and encouraging about her travel prospects, they worked out a support system for while she would be away and the next day, she drove into the programme without any fear of being in a car.

This is also an excellent example of how everything happens for us to learn from. The conscious mind was telling this lady that she had a fear of cars but her subconscious knew that she had developed that as a guilt free way of not being a 'bad daughter'. Once her imagination gave her this realisation, the fear disappeared and her relationship with her parents also improved.

This is why the imagination is such a powerful way for us to clear from our stuff. It doesn't teach us coping mechanisms, which are short term in enabling us to do the things we are fearful of – treating the symptoms, it allows us to get right to the root cause of the problem/ fear and without reliving it, change how we feel about it.

I have worked with people who have started this whole process with severe stress related aches and pains in their bodies. I have even worked with individuals who are so angry about something that has happened in their past that they described themselves as being constantly in pain. Their muscles having tightened and ultimately spasmed because of the emotional stress they had been feeling. For most of these people, even successfully being able to relax into one imagination journey can lessen the pain as the subconscious releases and heals.

We can't change what has happened in the past, but we can change our perception of what has happened and therefore our current experience of that reality. Combining the Shine philosophies of learning vs blaming and empowering ourselves through our imaginations to take 100% responsibility for what we are creating leads to truly sustainable personal transformation and a much more effortless, stress and pain free way of living.

Not only is the imagination a beautiful and fun place to heal and learn about ourselves, it is also, as already mentioned, the source of true original thought and creativity. A child can pick up a stick and a box and immediately be transported to a magical, mythical place that other children can jump into and share through their collective creative consciousness.

This is true up until the age of about seven when limiting beliefs begin to creep in and self-consciousness leads to doubt and starts to turn imagination into visualisation – ideas formed by what the child believes their peers/the world wants them to imagine, turning unique individual thought into creative adaption of what already exists. What they know to be safe.

This group think is what limits creativity in organisations and is Einstein's definition of insanity – "Doing the same thing over and over again and expecting different results."

To counter this and reintroduce our clients to using the imagination as a tool, we have developed a methodology we call Stem Cell Thinking, which is essentially a process to reimagine everything from a point of limitless possibility.

We first developed Stem Cell Thinking when we learned about the European Space Agency 'Moon and Mars Project'. We spent some time contemplating how to develop a thriving culture for humans to co-exist and contribute in health, harmony and love on a new planet without creating the same issues that we currently face as a species on Earth.

We realised that we have evolved to become expert problem solvers and chameleons, that we can learn from our experiences and adapt accordingly but that this often means that we limit possibility based on historic outcomes. We will also take the road most travelled in the mindset 'if it isn't broke, don't fix it'. This is why Kaizen and continuous improvement work so well in risk adverse cultures. True original thought is personally and organisationally risky – what if you make a mistake or fail? Our fear of consequences and of being wrong steers us away from using imagination.

Stem Cell Thinking does the absolute opposite. It only allows complete original thought, and strips out any limiting language or historic/cultural references (i.e. 'that won't happen here because…' or 'we tried that before and…') Participants start with a point of absolute zero and are not given any parameters to limit imagination except for the creation of a mission statement, question to be answered or goal for the process and even this is checked for any limiting beliefs or unconscious biases.

So, in the case of inhabiting Mars, the question could be 'How can we co-exist and contribute in a meaningful way that provides passion, purpose and unlocks individual and human potential?'

Using imagination through Stem Cell Thinking to answer this question could be the key to unlock what we need to do to transform our existence on this planet and all of the social, organisational and cultural eco-systems within it. I would be fascinated to bring three generations from around the world together to go through this process and see what truly unique ideas bubble out.

Homework:
Practice using your imagination as a tool for healing. Close your eyes and think of something or someone that is or has been triggering you or an ache or pain you have in your body. Listen to and feel how and where your body responds. What emotions come up? Does new pain appear? Does existing pain grow or change?

Once you are clear with how you are feeling, stand, sit or lie down and close your eyes. Connect with every part of your body and then relax and listen to one of the imagination journey audio files that you can download here XXXX.

Once the journey has finished, open your eyes and write down everything you can remember. There is no right or wrong way of doing this. If you didn't experience anything, it is OK. The imagination is a tool and like learning the guitar, needs to be practiced. If you fall asleep, that is also OK. Maybe your subconscious is telling you that you need to rest and rejuvenate rather than worry about the thing you are working on. If you do experience the journey, spend time noticing anything that was different on the way back to the start.

To finish, close your eyes and think of the something or someone that is or has been triggering you or the ache or pain you had in your body. Listen to and feel how and where your body responds. Is it the same or different to before? If it is different, something in your subconscious has changed and so have you.

The imagination journeys are also fantastic activities to do with children, especially if you are trying to get them to bed and to sleep. It is a great way of sharing thoughts and feelings in a non-threatening way and also to start the process of winding down and closing your eyes.

Notice what is different, not what is the same.

Anything Is Possible

Do you believe that anything is possible? Have a think about that for a moment and then ask yourself the question 'do you really believe it?' Not many people are able to truthfully answer yes for fear of being proven wrong and also a desire to not step too far away from reality and put ourselves 'out there'.

Most of us want to believe that anything is possible but we maintain a healthy dose of scepticism and the need for evidence before we will actually commit to believing. What we don't often realise however, is it can be this inability to step into the possibility that anything is possible that prevents us from actually doing or creating the very thing we are focussed on.

I have mentioned before that our beliefs are the most powerful part of our psyche. They determine who we are, what we do, how we look, feel and react and also what is possible for each of us in terms of potential. As humans we are born fully loaded with inherited beliefs from our families and also from history and culture. These beliefs are then developed and reaffirmed through parenting, education, our peers, mass media and marketing until we become full of self-limiting beliefs that erode our youthful confidence and fearless possibility.

As we get older this makes us feel like we are 'past our prime', 'too old' or that we have 'left it too late' and we take less risks and settle into comfortable patterns and routines that make us feel safe and purposeful. We think that because it has taken years to fully develop these limiting beliefs that it will take the same amount of years to change them or that it will never happen – you can't teach an old dog new tricks, right?

What is exciting to me about all of this is that the above simply isn't true. Our beliefs are electrical impulses and like energy can change in a second.

If I was to stand in front of you and tell you that I can flap my arms and fly, most of you wouldn't believe me at all. Some would laugh, others might feel concerned about me and there may even be a few that feel sorry for me – so certain in their belief that I am deluded or mad. I can pretty much guarantee that no one will say to me 'okay, go on then' and really mean it.

Our hard wiring to disbelieve and our desire to not be made a fool of kicks in immediately. What is beautiful about this is that if I then did actually start to move my arms in a vaguely wing like way and start to hover above the ground, every single person's belief system would instantly start to change. Of course, some would be looking for the strings or to see what the trick was but there would be an open minded few that feel something start to unlock inside themselves and may even have the confidence to lift their own arms and try it. Maybe just a few.

Now I am not saying that I can fly but I would rather be in the mindset that it is possible and open to it happening than not. It is the dreamers and the believers who live on an island and know there is something over the horizon that imagine and then build boats to take them there and see. These are the adventurers, the architects of our reality. Wouldn't you rather be one of those?

Isn't it true to say that absolutely everything was impossible at one time? If you go far enough back into history at some point you will find the time when the clothes you are wearing, the phone you are using, the food you are eating and the language you are speaking were impossible. No one knows what the future actually looks like. We can imagine and hypothesise but we can't say for sure and yet we are already programmed to limit our beliefs and therefore our evolution and potential.

Up until 1954 no one could run a mile in four minutes or under. We had been told by scientists and sports therapists that the human heart would explode if we ran that fast and this instilled belief was so powerful and so fear provoking that no one had been able change it until Roger Bannister did. He was not limited by this belief and was fearless in his challenge of it. Once Roger broke the record without his heart exploding, many other athletes did too and the record now sits at 3.43.13. The only thing that changed was the belief and the mindset and all of a sudden, the potential of the human as an athlete exponentially evolved.

The current world record for a person holding their breath underwater is 22 minutes and 22 seconds in 2012 by German free diver Tom Sietas which seems impossible right? When I was young, I was told that anyone underwater for seven minutes or longer would either die or have serious brain damage.

The recent fascination with exploring the limits of physical human possibility was inspired by the discovery of the Bajau tribe in Indonesia who have evolved to free dive to depths of 200 feet for as long as 13 minutes to catch fish. These nomadic people have developed larger spleens to enable them to spend so much time underwater which is scientifically seen as a mutation in their DNA but ultimately gives them a genetic advantage for life in the deep.

To the Bajau, this ability is normal and generations of their people have been born with the belief system that it is possible and therefore it is.

Wim Hoff is another example of defying limits of human possibility. Known as the 'Iceman', Hoff has developed the ability to withstand extreme cold and holds numerous Guinness World Records for swimming under and running barefoot on ice. He believes that he can regulate his body temperature to a degree that regardless of outside influences he can maintain a consistent core temperature.

As someone who massively feels the cold, I found this an interesting concept to explore further and challenge any disbelief I might have in my subconscious. So much so that in 2016 I spent 10-days at a retreat in Phuket which included daily ice baths. On the first day I couldn't even put my foot in

– the cold was such a shock that it hurt and I couldn't even imagine submerging myself in the water let alone staying in it. By day five I could stay in the bath for 20 minutes while resting my feet on a huge block of ice.

The only thing that changed in those five days was my belief that it was possible. Watching the other people at the spa do it and step out rejuvenated and revived helped me to stop seeing it as something horrible and painful and instead open my mind to the possibility that not only would it be good for me but that my body might actually need it. And with all of the May Thai and exercise I was doing – it did.

On Shine I ask the participants 'do you think you can heal yourself' which always creates an interesting discussion about what this actually means. In general, we know/believe that if we cut our finger, clean and dress it properly, in time it will heal. We may have a scar to remind us but the skin tissue will repair itself. Likewise, with a break, we know that for most people a broken bone that is reset and protected for a period of time will heal and become strong again.

What about if my arm is cut off – can I grow a new one? Currently the answer is no but why is this? There are species on earth like salamanders who can do exactly that? Is it just our belief system that is preventing us from healing ourselves to this extent?

The current world record for the number of babies to be born at a single birth is eight. Let's think about that for a minute. This means that with the aid of the sperm cell, a woman can create eight whole human beings in her body. Isn't that amazing? That is eight brains and hearts, eight skeletal and entire nervous systems, 16 lungs and 16 arms and legs. So why can't we regrow an arm or even the end of a finger if we lose one?

It excites me to contemplate this question. My belief and an offering to you is that the human body is completely created by what is happening in our minds. I believe that we don't have to exercise hard to be fit and toned and that we don't have to restrict what we eat (within reason) to be lean and healthy. I have a huge appetite and an active lifestyle full of travel. I also love to drink wine and eat cheese (I am a chee-gan – vegan that can't quite give up cheese!). I have sporadically been practising yoga for over 20 years and despite everything that the media tells us about what we need to do to be 'slim' I have a fit healthy body that can climb mountains, swim, surf and run without doing any of these things.

I truly think that this is down to my state of mind. I believe that I don't need to do much to maintain my fitness and my body (muscle memory) responds to this. Even if I haven't practiced yoga for four months, it only takes two 30-minute sessions for me to be able to go fully into the postures and for me to see the muscle tone and feel strong. I believe this is what every human is capable of and whether you agree or not – it is an exciting possibility.

You only have to look at the placebo and nocebo effects to see scientific evidence of the power of our minds over our bodies. If you are unfamiliar with the concepts, look them up. There are thousands of fascinating cases where volunteers in medical trials have unknowingly been given sugar tablets instead of real medication and told either that they will heal them in some way (placebo) or create physical side effects (nocebo) such as hair loss. In the majority of cases the sugar tablet has a similar effect to the real medication. Meaning that the volunteers taking the tablets have such a strong belief in what they have been told that they create this as a physical reality.

If you want to take this exploration even further have a look into Dissociative Identity Disorder – people diagnosed with this believe that they are more than one person and often have multiple personalities. There is evidence to show that individuals switching between personalities can have drastic physical changes such as severe allergies in one personality that are not there in another. Often personalities will completely change posture and therefore height and size, handwriting style and artistic/physical abilities.

The recent film Split takes this exploration to the extreme but for me it also encourages my curiosity and open minded-ness about the link between mindset (belief) and our physical reality.

It also fascinates me that we have merely scratched the surface of what we are capable of mentally and that we may only be utilising up to 10% of our brains, arguably the most complicated and powerful living organism on the planet. I love watching films such as Lucy and Limitless which explore the bringing together of all consciousness so that every single sentient being on the planet can access absolutely everything that has ever been thought, felt, experienced, seen, heard, smelled, tasted and imagined. The exploration of which is thought by many to be an amazing fantasy.

One of my personal missions in life is to unlock the true potential of the human and I have dedicated my career to this both through the work that I do with leadership and personal development in organisations and also through our Three Global Goals.

Having an open mind and stepping into the possibility that anything is possible is an important part of this journey and I am excited to see what we are capable of creating and doing with a truly limitless mindset.

If we re-imagine education and learning so that it taps into passion and purpose and empower everyone with limitless possibility, we can create non-judgemental, fear-less environ-ments where anything is possible. Imagine an education sys-tem that encourages and empowers future generations to be-lieve that they can do or be anything. Even if they are reaching for the moon and find the stars, everything in our global eco-system will change.

As far as I can see, based on how my life is unfolding, there is no downside to believing that anything is possible. Every day I wake up excited about further unlocking my po-tential and I am constantly stepping outside of my comfort zone and enjoying everything that this creates for me.

At the age of 12 when I was in a hammock in the back garden of our council house with my younger sister looking at the stars and imagining how I could change the world, I didn't have any idea that I would become the co-founder of a global company transforming lives and traveling the world but I did believe that I could do absolutely anything I set my mind to and I am.

Homework:

Ask yourself the question 'Do I believe anything is possible?' and see what comes up in your mind, emotions and body. How does that question make you feel? Do you have reservations? Scepticism? How has reading this chapter made you feel?

Then do something brave. Think of something that you have been meaning or wanting to do but have allowed your beliefs that you can't do it or that it won't be possible to stop you. Write it down and list all the reasons why you can and should do it. Identify what you need and any support required. Create an action plan for the first steps towards it and do it. If your journey is anything like mine, you will feel amazing and as your confidence grows you will do this more and more. The only thing that limits us in life is us.

Notice what is different, not what is the same.

Whole-Body Listening Movement

The World Health Organisation has stated that currently a quarter of the world's population is 'not active enough to stay healthy'. Around 1.4 billion adults spend the majority of their time sitting at desks all day at work, in front of the TV in the evening and travelling by car.

The level of obesity is on the rise and people are getting sicker and more reliant than ever on pharmaceutical drugs and holistic therapies to reduce the physical symptoms of this inactivity and emotional stress.

Our bodies are designed to move. They are also a sophisticated and complex communication system, taking in and providing information to our brain every single second. They are constantly talking to us and letting us know what we are thinking, feeling and experiencing but most people are unaware of this.

We currently exist in a cerebral world where the majority of our focus and attention is on what we are thinking, feeling, seeing, hearing, smelling and physical touch. We believe that these are the significant inputs helping us to make choices and experience the world without realising that there is so much more information for us to tap into.

Every cell in our body is a receptor and communicator through the language of chemical signals. Hormones and neurotransmitters act like words, telling a cell about the environment around it. For example, when you eat, your pancreas releases insulin to tell the other cells in the body to remove glucose from the blood. It is an internal biological conversation similar to our mouths communicating with our ears.

In the same way, our emotions create the release of chemicals in our bodies such as adrenalin and serotonin based on how we are feeling – our bodies are listening and responding accordingly. When we are stressed or anxious our bodies release hormones that trigger our 'fight or flight' response. Our breath quickens, heart starts to race and our muscles tighten ready for action. If the perceived fear or stressful situation goes then the hypothalamus should tell our body to return to normal but if the stressor doesn't go away the response will continue.

Last year, the Mental Health Foundation conducted the largest known study of stress levels in the UK and found that 74% of people have felt so stressed that they have been completely overwhelmed and unable to cope. Contributors to this included debt, long-term health issues, the need to be like everyone else or 'fit in' and body image issues.

Just imagine the impact this will be having on our bodies. When the mind is stressed, we release hormones to tense our muscles and when the stress doesn't go, they stay like that. This creates tension, aches, pains and can lead to longer term, more serious physical issues both internally and externally if we don't listen to what our bodies are telling us.

If my shoulders are sore and I realise I am holding them up and tense, I know that they didn't raise by themselves. Something happened that affected me emotionally and my body responded to let me know this. My shoulders aren't hurting and creating stress in my neck to sabotage my ability to do things, they are talking to me and letting me know what I am feeling.

When you think about this for a moment you will realise how amazing it is. The problem is that most people have forgotten how to listen. We have become experts at either dealing with the pain or using coping mechanisms such as pain killers, exercise, massage, alcohol and drugs to mask the pain and allow us to continue.

We are so good at masking pain from ourselves that often we don't even realise it is there. For example, when we check in on Shine and participants have their eyes closed to connect to the body, they often feel pain that they hadn't noticed or remembered until that moment. What is interesting is that pain is always there but the coping mechanisms created to 'overcome' can be powerful enough to mask it and allow us to carry on until the message becomes louder.

I have worked with people who believe that pain is normal and believe it will always be there. Imagine the impact this will be having on the entire nervous system, eventually leading to adrenal fatigue.

Stress related physical ailments start as a whisper. Headaches, tension in the neck and shoulders, tiredness and digestion issues are all our bodies' way of telling us that our hormones are out of balance. When we don't listen to the whisper it will eventually become a shout so that we have to do something about it.

Most of us know people who have waited until they have become extremely sick or incapacitated before listening to their body and changing their lifestyle. They have needed a medical scare or a dramatic physical change to help them to understand that our bodies are teaching us about our environments and our emotional state of being.

The good news is that once you fully understand and embrace this concept, you don't need to wait for the shout. You can listen to the whisper and ask yourself what your body is teaching you.

I am often asked on Shine how to start the process of listening to your body again when we are so used to trying to prevent the pain signals from reaching our minds and my answer is first of all to reconnect. Close your eyes and put your intention slowly into every part of your body from the tips of your toes to the top of your head and ask yourself what you are feeling.

Allow your neurotransmitters to do their work and listen to what your body is telling you.

Another way of doing this is through movement. Stand up, walk, run, dance, play – allow your body to move freely and without force and see what messages it gives to you. Our muscles store emotional memories and when we move and stretch, we can release them.

This is why getting a deep tissue massage when you have been through a traumatic time can make you feel emotional. I have cried my eyes out on the massage table a number of times and felt so much calmer and centred afterwards without even knowing consciously what the experience was that created the emotion in the first place.

According to neuropharmacologist, Candace Pert, 'The body is our subconscious mind' and unexpressed emotions are literally lodged in the body. If this is true, it means that every time we feel guilty, angry or sad and don't allow ourselves to express this, we can store the emotion in our body and create tension and pain, often in a place that is relevant to the emotion.

In traditional Chinese medicine, emotions and physical health are intimately connected. Sadness, anxiety and fear are each associated with a particular area or organ in the body.

For example, grief and worry can affect lung function and anger can affect the liver.

I also believe that the external physical symptoms we experience are speaking to us in a way that is obvious when you open your mind to asking the questions 'why am I creating this and what is it telling me'. Pain in the back of the neck and the feeling of sore, heavy shoulders can represent the weight of the world. Leg injuries or pain can represent fear of change or movement. Whether this is true or not, asking yourself these questions will create a mindset that is much more likely to hear the answers you need to change and ultimately to heal.

Most of us lead such sedentary lives these days that even the thought of standing up for any length of time makes us feel tired and going to the gym to 'exercise' is something we believe we have to do to stay fit. Bringing movement into your life in whatever form you feel comfortable will help you to stay connected to your body and allow your cellular communication system to work more effectively.

The next time you experience a headache or pain in your body, rather than reaching for the paracetamol, ask yourself what your body is telling you.

According to New Vision, dehydration is a leading cause of diseases and symptoms can range from mild to life threatening. For example, dehydration can cause inflammation throughout the body which can lead to medical conditions such as asthma, arthritis, high blood pressure, cancer and obesity. If this is true, simply drinking more water can completely change how you feel.

I have truly embraced the concept of whole-body listening and in the last four years I haven't needed to visit a doctor at all. Anytime I have felt myself getting sick or have had pain I have asked myself why I have created it, listened to the answer and acted on it. Most of the time I either need to drink more water, eat more healthily or have some guilt free rest.

Why do you think a massive proportion of the population gets a cold as soon as winter comes and not during the summer months? It seems obvious to me that when it's cold, wet and dark outside most of us would like to stay in bed with a hot chocolate, Netflix or a good book. This doesn't mean that we are pretending to be ill or consciously wanting the flu but our bodies are listening to our subconscious needs and desires and our bodies are reflecting this to us.

I know plenty of people who always get sick when they take holiday and I feel that one of the reasons for this is that they feel guilty for allowing themselves time to rest or have fun.

I'm sure this resonates with at least some of you reading.

If you want to take this concept even further like I have, there are sometimes subconscious reasons for creating pain or discomfort that without increased awareness are difficult to make the connections to. When I was in South Africa recently, I was bitten by a spider which resulted in an allergic reaction and ultimately in me calling my mum for advice. My stepdad answered the phone as my mum was out walking the dog and when I asked if he was OK? Confided in me that he had been having excruciating headaches for some days. This led to me

118

insisting on him getting a scan at which point we discovered that he had another bleed on his brain and he was rushed to hospital for surgery.

My belief system is that I needed to not only get bitten by the spider but have an extreme allergic reaction otherwise I wouldn't have called my mum, spoken to my stepdad and ultimately ensured that he sought treatment. He hadn't told my mum about the headaches as he didn't want to worry her.

Whether this resonates with you or not, there is no downside to exploring all of the reasons why you can have created the pain or illness. Rather than seeing it as bad and getting upset and angry, it means you are in a mindset of learning what your body is telling you and are therefore much more likely to not need the pain anymore and heal faster.

Whole-body listening will help you to feel more connected, centred and in control of your health and ultimately your wellbeing. Physical movement enhances this process and also increases blood flow, metabolism and cell/brain regeneration.

I describe myself as a kinetic being when I am on programme and what I mean by this is that I believe motion and movement are paramount to my ability to not only connect with myself and others but also to generate ideas and be in absolute feminine flow. The literal definition of kinetic is to have the ability to harness the power of kinesis (motion) within one's self which some believe empowers you to connect with and learn from the collective consciousness.

I don't know if this is true but whether I am running, dancing, hiking or making love, I feel that movement transcends the need for language. That my subconscious is able to speak to me through my body without the need for analysis that my conscious mind so often creates.

Homework:

Stand up or lie down somewhere quiet and on your own without any distraction and spend time putting your awareness into every part of your body. Think about the part and then relax and allow it to speak to you. Is there any pain or unusual feeling? If so, what emotions come up? Does it make you think of anyone or anything? You can use the imagination journey and process to see if it changes and then examine if the feeling is the same or different.

Next time you get a headache or feel a sudden pain close your eyes and ask yourself the question 'what just happened or what did I just think about that may have caused it?'. Even if the answer doesn't come to your conscious mind, you might just find that the pain disappears without you needing to take any tablets.

Schedule some kind of movement into your life every week, whether it is going for a walk, dancing to music as you cook dinner or starting a new physical hobby. Remember that our bodies are meant to move and by liberating them from the constraint of sitting all of the time, they are much more likely to speak to you.

Notice what is different, not what is the same.

Passions and Purpose

Joseph Campbell said 'Follow your bliss – find what you love doing and are passionate about and do more of it' and what I think he meant by this is that human beings are meant to be happy. Our short time on this earth is meant to be filled with awe and wonder and contribution that makes us feel empowered and enriched.

Being in a state of happiness feels effortless, it is energising and rejuvenating because our serotonin levels increase. Being stressed, angry or sad creates cortisol which helps our body to adapt to stress in the short term but in the long term it lowers our serotonin levels which leaves us feeling like our energy has been drained and can create illness and pain.

With this is mind, why don't we spend the majority of our time doing things that we love to do? Why is it that when I ask participants on my programmes what their passion is, most of them have absolutely no idea?

I have recently been inspired and moved by the story of the late Claire Wineland who had Cystic Fibrosis and died after a double lung transplant when she was only 21. She spent her entire life knowing that death was imminent and because of this lived every day seeking happiness and doing the things that she was passionate about.

She didn't get caught up in the treadmill of existing, of waiting for that thing to happen before she allowed herself to wholeheartedly enjoy life. She didn't wait for that job, or house, to find true love or reach a certain weight. She saw her situation as a blessing and used her short time to speak up about the things she wanted to change in the world and to immerse herself in every moment that she had with those that she loved.

If you watch her YouTube videos you will see that despite being close to death, Claire radiated life and was guilt free in following her bliss.

It really made me think about the society we have created and whether our fear of death is so great that we spend all of our time focused on not dying and being safe and secure in our houses, jobs and relationships rather than on truly living.

What Claire has taught me is when you know that you are going to die and it is inevitable you can get on with enjoying every moment of living and I think this is the same for relationships. If you exist in the paradigm that the relationship can be over at any given moment you can truly experience and appreciate the delicious passion, desire and wonderment of being with that person then.

People talk about living every day as if it is your last but because it is said so many times and in so many ways, I don't think that people really realise the full impact of what this means. When you think of it in the context of relationships it truly makes sense. Every day we take for granted the people we love. We assume that they will be there forever or at least for as long as we can imagine and so we take out our frustrations on them, we try and change them from the beautiful unique people they are into the people that we and society think that they should be. We stifle and berate them, we stop listening to their dreams and their energy, we forget to look into their eyes and fully experience the amazing beings that they are.

It's like saving crystal glasses for a special occasion and then you die, what is more special than right now? We should be drinking our morning orange juice from those glasses and delighting in the way they catch the sun light and make it dance on the wall.

When Steve Jobs was close to death, he shared that his greatest regrets were not spending enough time with the people he loved, doing the things that he enjoyed. I believe that this would be true for most human beings and while it is important to have access to the things that we need to sustain life and live comfortably, we often prioritise wealth and recognition over health and happiness.

When did you last give time to yourself or someone you love without checking your phone, thinking about the things that you need to or should be doing? When was the last time that you did absolutely nothing and just enjoyed the sounds, feelings and sensations you experience?

I used to think that doing nothing was lazy and it was hilarious for my friends and family to watch me try and 'relax'. There are so many awkward pictures of me lying on a sun bed or sitting trying to do nothing as it felt completely alien to my constant state of movement and my belief system that if I was doing nothing that I was wasting time.

Now I understand that to find what we love doing and are passionate about, we need to allow ourselves time to first relax and stop consciously thinking so that our subconscious can speak to us. This relaxation doesn't have to be being still, it can be cooking, eating, watching movies, drinking nice wine, drawing, dancing, laughing, sleeping, imagining, meditating. Whatever it is that you do that makes your whole body relax and allows you to stop worrying and thinking about the future. It will be the thing that brings you to now.

I find that the rhythm of practicing yoga or swimming works well, it is like a meditation and because I am focused on the physical part of the action, I am not consciously thinking about anything else. This creates space for my subconscious to speak. Once in that relaxed state you can ask yourself the question 'what is it that I love to do?' and see what happens.

The beauty of this process is that you don't need to get an answer or realisation immediately, by simply asking the question you are opening yourself to the possibility that there is something that you are passionate about. For some people this will be the first time you have even asked yourself this question.

We get so caught up in the patterns of life and what we consciously think we should have achieved by certain ages that we forget to give ourselves the time and space to work on being happy. Most people I ask about this tie happiness and contentment to success and recognition without even knowing what success actually means to them.

When thinking about what being successful means, it is easy to get stuck in the limitations of what we currently have rather than the possibility of what we can create in the future.

Of those few that do know what they love to do, a high proportion don't believe that they can actually make money doing it, which simply isn't true. You can make money, or better still create value, doing absolutely anything if you are creative about it and in an open limitless mindset.

A great example is my brother-in-law Ben who is absolutely passionate about building and flying drones which he was previously doing as an expensive hobby. At this time, he didn't believe that he could possibly do this for a living. After some coaching, he decided to borrow money to buy a laser cutter that would not only allow him to efficiently and professionally build the drones but also to create furniture and other saleable items which helped to fund his passion.

The creation of RoundTable Global is my personal example of 'following your bliss'. I have co-created a business that is financially successful and sustainable at the same time as enabling me to pursue my passion for educational innovation, empowering everyone and environmental rejuvenation – our Three Global Goals. In addition to this I get to travel, be creative, speak and work with friends, family and people who inspire me on a daily basis.

What is even more beautiful about the life I have created for myself, is that the young people in my eco-system are being inspired to find their passions and sense of purpose and pursue them. By being happy and following your bliss, you are giving permission to others to do the same. It goes back to what I have been saying about the power of our beliefs, what you believe you create.

In one of her videos, Claire Wineland asks the question 'how can you make your life beautiful?' and I think this is a question that we all need to ponder, even if we can't answer it immediately. She also asks if 'you are proud of the life you are living?' which is something I now ask myself whenever I check in and I will think about when I make decisions for myself and for the company.

To make this process easier, take money out of the thought process. Pretend for a moment that you don't need any money or that it doesn't exist. According to the ex-missionary Daniel Everett, the happiest people in the world are the primitive Pirahã tribe in Brazil. These people live a simple life completely off grid, grow their own food and exchange their skills for the things that they need. In comparison to the western world, they have nothing but, in their minds, they have everything.

My own experience in the 15 years that I have been traveling and living around the world is similar. I have found that those who seem to have the least can be the happiest. As long as they have food, shelter, company and the ability to contribute and connect, their lives seem full of love and laughter.

The simpler life is, the more it can be filled with pleasure and passion. The more complicated life is, the more time we have to spend doing everything and thinking about keeping things going in the future. It is the same with money, those with the most money seem to spend more time worrying more about losing it whereas those with nothing give freely.

Many of us think that recognition and reward will fulfil our sense of purpose but I have found that it's what we are creating that matters – it is what we are contributing to this world and the global eco-system that fills us with joy.

Finding what you are passionate about could mean standing up for the things that you believe in, it could mean becoming a singer or songwriter. Whatever it is, it fills you with energy and enthusiasm, it motivates you to do more and to become the best version of yourself.

Why would you live a life where you dread getting out of bed in the morning when you can wake up excited with the possibility of your day? I believe that everyone has a reason for being on this Earth and whether that is to simply enjoy the feel of the sun on your skin or to invent a cure for cancer, we are all connected and our collective happiness is significant in the evolution of human kind.

Being happy and having passion and purpose might just be the very thing that enables us to change the way that we currently exist in the global eco-system and we can move from surviving to truly thriving.

Homework:

What have been the happiest moments of your life? What were you doing? Who with? How did you feel? Write them down and spend time remembering every part of the experience. Share them with people that you love and ask them the same questions. Doing this will release more serotonin into your system and help you to relax.

Think back to when you were a child, what did you love doing? What did you want to do with your life? What were your dreams? Allow yourself time to do these things again, even if they feel uncomfortable or silly. Playing isn't just for children, it is a way of practicing and honing skills and talents in a risk-free environment.

Spend time with young people and ask them what they love to do. Ask yourself the questions above and then go on an imagination journey and see if your subconscious speaks to you.

Remember that if you are creative and step into the possibility that anything is possible, you can follow your bliss to your passion and purpose.

Notice what is different, not what is the same.

Live Your Dream

I am so excited for everyone reading this book who is giving themselves the gift of time to go through the Shine journey. Having taken 1000s of people through the programme in person and being privileged to hold the space and see their transformations, I know that when the messages and philosophies resonate and land, there is potential for much personal change to happen.

The strap-line of this book is 'Effortless Abundance and Unconditional Love' and this is my mantra for living. It is what I wish for each and every one of you and for every person on the planet. I know that this will come when we each take 100% responsibility for what we are co-creating and have an open, limitless learning mindset.

I truly believe that life does not have to be hard, that we don't have to make mistakes to learn or fail to succeed and that we can all create a reality where we are living our dreams, whatever they may be and however big or small they are. The RoundTable Global team and I are proof that this is possible.

But first you need to spend time identifying what your dream is and learn not to be attached to it becoming a reality in the way that you expect it to. Having a big gnarly dream that you are attached to is exciting but it can also be limiting. I believe it is the same as have a business plan or a strategy. If I decide and commit to a certain amount of growth or revenue generation by a certain time frame, then I may be energetically limiting the company from exceeding this.

When we started RoundTable, we didn't create a strategy, instead we committed to our Three Global Goals (Educational Innovation, Empowering Everyone and Environmental Rejuvenation) and we spent time thinking about the lifestyle we each wanted to create for ourselves (flexible working, travel, ability to follow other passions, abundance). This has freed us up to naturally follow the flow of where the business has taken us and has exceeded our wildest expectations.

In just four years we have grown to be able to deliver programmes in 20 different countries. We are working with some of the biggest organisations in the world. We are profitable and able to sustain our charitable giving through these profits and we have over 100 leaders, activists and influencers representing 26 different countries helping us to deliver our Three Global Goals as Ambassadors for Change. These include First Ladies, singers, actors, film makers, CEOs, inspirational young people and policy makers. Oh, and we have been winning awards for our work since year two.

Isn't that amazing? When people ask me about RoundTable and I tell our story, I realise just how unique our growth and business model is. Had we have created a plan or a strategy, we wouldn't have been in the mindset to create the things that have emerged organically and effortlessly for us.

This mindset is useful when you are thinking about what your dream is and how you want to live your life.

When I ask participants on Shine what they want to be in the world or what it is that they want to achieve, most find it easier to tell me what they don't want. They will say things like 'well I don't want to work nine to five anymore' or 'I don't want to attract in another relationship like the last one'. My belief is that the universal energy, or collective consciousness doesn't know the difference between 'want' and 'don't want' so when we spend time focused on what we don't want, we are feeding that energy and much more likely to attract it in.

This is why it is important for us to focus on what we do want. The best way of starting this process is for you to think about how you want to spend your minutes, hours, days, weeks and years. Be selfish. Step into your masculine and imagine what you would like to do if you could every day. It may be that initially you'd like to sleep or get more rest because your body feels tired and that is OK. Think ahead to the future and imagine yourself refreshed and rejuvenated, what would you be doing? Would you like to do that alone or with someone else or other people?

When you think about your relationship or significant other, rather than make a list of the things you would like them to be or have, think about how you would like to spend your time and how being with another person could enhance this.

By focusing on self and what you love to do, you are much more likely to attract in the resources, opportunities and people that will help to make this possible. Remember that we are energetic beings and that what we broadcast out, we attract in. We feel each other and subconsciously respond.

If you love to travel and are focused on creating a life of adventure and exploration, you are much more likely to attract in likeminded people who share that passion. Even spending time thinking about it and allowing yourself to dream and imagine will start the process.

For the rest of this chapter, I am going to take you through a process of identifying your dream or personal goal. This is something that you can do alone but also works really well with another person or even with a group as you can then help, challenge and coach each other. Just be aware as you go through the process that we are not creating something that is set in stone, this is the start of a journey towards imagining what you want and the life you want to live. Be open to change and to your dreams coming true in ways that you never imagined.

I live my life aware of push and pull. If I feel that I am having to chase or push for something to happen then I know either the timing isn't right or that it isn't supposed to happen. If something is effortlessly pulling me in a certain direction such as a new unexpected opportunity, I know that I have subconsciously attracted it to take me closer to learning, changing and personal happiness. This being in flow is the feminine energy side of living your dream. Be aware if you are being rigid and attached to expectations.

For this process you will need paper and something to write with.

First of all, stand up and connect to your body. Take your intention from the soles of your feet all the way up your body to the top of your head and be aware of your breathing and of relaxing every part of you before you start. Move if you need to. Allow your body to speak to you. Think about creating a dream. How does that feel? What emotions come up? What beliefs come into your mind? Allow everything to come without resistance and write down anything you want to remember.

For the next part I usually use four pieces of uplifting music without lyrics but you can do it in silence if you prefer.

Sit down, close your eyes again, take a deep breath and connect again to your body. Think of the word 'Health'. When you are ready, open your eyes, press play on the first piece of music and spend the time until it finished writing down everything that health and being healthy means to you. It can be a list or a stream of consciousness. Don't think too hard about it, just write. You should aim for between three to five minutes for this and each of the next words.

When you are finished, either naturally or because the music ends, close your eyes again, take a deep breath and connect to the body. Think of the word 'Love'. Open your eyes, start the next piece of music or the timer and start to write. What does the word love mean to you? How does it make you feel? Who or what do you think of? Continue until the music or the timer ends.

Repeat this process for the words 'Life' and 'Work'. Don't think too much, allow yourself to be in flow. Be honest and authentic. Notice if any emotions come to the surface, any thoughts or memories. Write them down without analysis and in the knowledge that you are allowing your subconscious to speak to you.

When you are finished, go for a walk or do something to break the energy. When you feel ready, return to what you have written and read it through. If you are going through the process alone, highlight or underline the things that stand out or you feel a strong resonance or emotion towards. If you are with someone else, share your words with each other and ask each other questions to further explore what you have written.

Once you are ready, put the writing aside and use a new clean piece of paper. Close your eyes, deep breath, connect to your body and with or without music when you open them write at the top of the paper 'Empower Self'. Then spend five minutes writing in the free flow of consciousness, all of the things that you are going to do as a direct result of reading this book to empower yourself.

When you are finished, close your eyes again, deep breath, connect to the body and when you open your eyes write 'Empower Others'. Spend another five minutes writing down all of the things that you are going to do to empower others as a result of your journey through Shine.

After the time is up, go for a walk or do something else to break the energy. When you are ready, return and repeat the process as before. If alone, read what you have written and see what you notice. Highlight priorities and actions that really resonate. If with someone else, share and help each other to identify what is important to you.

Pick up to three things or actions from your 'Empower Self' and 'Empower Others' writing and spend some time thinking about how these can help you to start to live your dream. Is it obvious from what you have written what you want to do and how you want to spend your time?

Are there commitments to actions that you can create for each of these? What would be your next steps? For each thing or action, you identify think about the following; what are the skills, resources, support systems and opportunities that you already have that can help you to deliver them? What are the skills, resources, support systems and opportunities that you need to create to be able to deliver them?

Think about who may be able to help you or what you need to do to start the journey. Capture everything and then allow yourself to sleep on it. Remember that you are creating a dream or goals that will empower you to start the journey towards personal happiness, not a rigid plan that you must stick to and follow.

Before you go to sleep, connect to your body and think of what you have committed to. Do you feel anything in your body? Does anything come up? Have your dream or actions in your mind and listen to one of the imagination journeys.

If you fall asleep, when you wake up check in with yourself and your dream or actions and see if they are different, need adding to or amending. If you don't fall asleep, when you have finished the imagination journey ask yourself the same questions. Make notes if you need to.

Go to sleep knowing that you have started the journey towards realising your dreams, even if those dreams are not what you consciously thought they might be, they could just be so much more.

Homework:

As this chapter is already taking you through a process there is no homework except for when you are ready, to start to share your dreams and plans. The more you speak them out loud and the more you share with others in your eco-system, the more you will broadcast out energy towards attracting them.

This whole chapter is also a lovely process that you can take other people through, especially loved ones and your children. Enjoy! Notice what is different, not what is the same.

Beyond Sustainability
Personal Impact

I have written Shine as an offering to empower and educate through the knowledge and philosophies we have collectively created at RoundTable which is in alignment with two of our Three Global Goals. I feel it is important to also share with you our thinking around goal three – Environmental Rejuvenation as I feel that it is imperative that we take collective responsibility for what we are creating in our global eco-system.

I constantly hear people talking about the need to 'save our planet' and from our perspective this focus needs adjusting. It is arrogant to think that as a species we can destroy Earth, a planet that has existed for millions of years. Whatever humans do, once we are gone, slowly but surely the Earth will rejuvenate. It may take millions more years and may have a completely different biosphere and therefore eco-system but the likelihood is that it will naturally restore itself and create a new balance for the species that remain or evolve.

At RoundTable, we think the focus should be on saving ourselves and what we mean by that is our ability to continue to exist on this beautiful planet. We need collective understanding that we are the only species intentionally destroying our natural habitat and if we don't change this – we won't have anything left.

Every single other sentient being on the planet exists in a symbiotic, healthy and balanced way. When lions hunt, they kill what they need as a pride to feed and leave the rest for the jackals, hyenas and birds of prey to pick at. Then they rest and kill/feed again when they need to. In my time traveling the world and specifically through Africa, I've never seen an obese lion, or any food going to waste.

I was born as a vegetarian and yet I am not against people that eat meat. What I work towards changing is the quantity that is consumed and the way that the animals are bred and the lives they lead before they are consumed.

I feel strongly that the meat and dairy industries currently have a huge destructive impact on the planet through deforestation, the food and water required to keep the livestock alive and also methane emissions. In addition to this, energetically speaking, I can't help but think that the inhumane way that much of this livestock is killed is having an impact on our collective consciousness.

In the same way that we feel the pain of other people suffering, we must also feel the pain of other sentient beings.

Where ever you stand on this point, the move towards a more plant-based diet for all has got to be in the best interest of sustaining our natural habitat and therefore our ability to continue to live on this planet. Even if those that continue to eat meat, fish and insects, do so in a more ethical way, our impact on the world will lessen.

Because of this we have created the concept of 'Beyond Sustainability'. To sustain is to continue things as they currently are without change but we believe that we need to go beyond this and create leadership action to restore and rejuvenate the eco-system. If we sustain things the way they are now, with our current rate of consumption and consumerism, we will eventually run out of food and resources.

We believe that we need to think creatively about solutions that rejuvenate and provide opportunities to change the way that we interact with our world. This is why we have funded and developed Beyond Bamboo (www.BeyondBamboo.online) as one of our Three Global Goal initiatives.

Beyond Bamboo is our attempt and commitment to creating conscious and ethical consumerism in a virtual, accessible online marketplace. Not only have we launched it as a global hub where people can explore this concept and find inspiring resources and knowledge, it is also a marketplace full of beautiful, ethical products.

Each of our partners were approached based on their ability to work towards being 'Beyond Sustainable' and we are committed to coach them to further develop this.

Being plant based, we found it difficult to find one place where we could buy all the things that we needed, so we have created one. Beyond Bamboo is still relatively new and we are officially launching the UK marketplace at Vegan Life in London just next week, but the concept it exciting and for us demonstrates our commitment to changing relationships with consumerism.

Not only are our partners working towards being plant based, animal cruelty free, ethical and sustainable. Wherever possible we seek those that are contributing back to their local communities and therefore in alignment with our desire to bring triple bottom line reporting into everyday practice for organisations. They are delivering against measurable targets focused on people, planet and profit and if not, we will help them to do so.

In addition to this, we have also created 'Near You' as part of Beyond Bamboo which is currently being developed as a mobile phone app and can be used to find beyond sustainable products and services in major cities around the world. As part of Near You, we are also listing places where you can recycle, up-cycle, exchange, purchase second hand goods and spend time with like-minded, conscious consumers.

We are offering our customers options to not buy new products if they don't have to or want to and also to exchange what they do have without spending money where possible.

We are really excited about Beyond Bamboo and the potential it creates for us to not only make the concept of being 'Beyond Sustainable' mainstream, but also to engage with people around the world who want to make a more conscious lifestyle choice and need help and inspiration to do this.

Taking 100% responsibility for your life, also means taking 100% responsibility for your ability to continue to exist and thrive on this planet. This means firstly becoming aware of your personal impact on the eco-system and then taking individual leadership action towards not just reducing this but to restore and rejuvenate through making new conscious choices wherever possible.

Homework:

Spend some time thinking about the things that you do that have an impact on the environment such as travel, what you consume, what you buy, what you throw away and how you dispose of it.

What different choices could you make?

Can you walk, cycle or run some of the time rather than always take transport that requires fuel? Could you go plant based one day a week? Would you consider going to a charity shop the next time you need to buy something? There are also hundreds of local online resources listing free furniture and resources that other people no longer want – can you make it a practice to look there before buying new? Are there charities near you that are up-cycling and reconditioning old products and furniture? Can you take reusable straws, food ware and napkins with you when you have to eat out or take away? Are you recycling your waste? Are there ways to reduce your waste? Can you grow your own food?

Our dream is that eventually Beyond Bamboo will have all of this information and capability in one place for you and if you absolutely have to buy – we will have already put in the work to ensure that anything you purchase through the site, you can feel good about.

Notice what is different, not what is the same.

Solo Reflection

This chapter of Shine is to remind you to spend time reflecting on everything you are learning and to give yourself permission to be alone with your thoughts and feelings. Unlike meditation which can be focused on emptying the mind and being still, the solo reflection is a time for you to listen and learn from your inner dialogue.

It will be useful but not absolutely essential, to do this after every chapter if you can.

Find a space somewhere that you can be alone and without distraction, preferably outside in nature and make sure that you don't have your phone or any electrical devices with you.

Take only paper and something to write with.

Go for a walk, sit and look at a beautiful view or sunrise/sunset, return to a place that means something to you, put your bare feet in the grass/sand/water. Be somewhere that you feel is relevant to your journey. This is a time just for you.

Once you are comfortably in that space, whether moving, standing or sitting, give yourself at least ten minutes of just being. Notice everything around you. What can you see, hear, smell and feel? What colours jump out? Focus your attention on something specific and see if you notice more with that focus.

When you feel ready, close your eyes, take a deep breath, connect slowly to your body from your feet to your head. Notice how your body feels, do you have any aches or pains? If so, when you focus on them what comes into your thoughts? What emotions do you feel? Acknowledge them, write them down if you need to and then move your focus elsewhere.

When this process feels complete to you, open your eyes and take another deep breath as you look at your surroundings.

Think about the chapter you have just read or the entire journey you have been on through Shine so far. What has resonated with you? What has felt the most impactful? What has changed for you and how has your eco-system responded and changed? What have you learned about yourself? What questions do you have that still need answering? What actions would you like to take? What did you find challenging and what do you need to better understand or find out more about?

Capture anything you feel you would like to remember or do and then continue to enjoy the space you have created for yourself for as long as feels right to you.

Your Time to Shine

It is an absolute privilege and a commitment to my calling to be able to share with you all the philosophies of Shine. I am in awe of the people who have taken the leap to go through this journey and I am constantly humbled by the stories of transformation and deep learning that are shared with me.

When I first started this process of stepping into authenticity and responsibility, I can remember being full of fear that I would forget what I had been taught or that with time I would fall back into my old patterns and paradigms.

Like any skill, it has taken practice and immersion for me to get to a place where I can take 100% responsibility for and learn from everything that I create. There were times when I was utterly frustrated with my inability to stop blaming or looking outside of myself for answers.

This may happen for you, or it may not. Either way, be gentle with yourself and know that like the famous Ralph Waldo Emerson saying – 'Life is a journey, not a destination' and so is Shine. Enjoy traveling the path you have chosen and as much as you can focus on and learn from each step and milestone as they unfold, rather than rushing towards what you think will be the end.

You and your eco-system are constantly growing, changing and evolving and as such you will create opportunities to challenge and open your mindset and to step courageously out of your comfort zone. Each of which may require you to learn again or alter your perception of what you have already learned.

What I will say is that as your personal story and journey reveals itself to you, everything you need to continue your change is in this book. We have designed Shine so that you can return to relevant chapters and remind yourself of the philosophies whenever you need to.

I am constantly doing this. The writing of this book has been a beautiful journey of personal re-immersion and further development of everything that we are offering. In every chapter I have learned something new about myself and changed in some way.

I have had aha moments and some of the philosophies have landed in new and different ways which I know have helped me to better explain them to you.

The more you can immerse yourself in Shine, the easier the journey will become. I also found that introducing the concepts and philosophies to those in my eco-system helped me to further embed and embrace the learning.

You may find that some of the chapters and philosophies don't resonate or make sense to you now but that if you re-read them in a month, a year, ten years' time they may be the perfect thing to help you understand how to learn from what you are creating then.

I have been through a lot personally in the months of writing Shine. I separated from my partner of four years at the same time as dealing with the tragic and accidental death of my father, who was one of my closest friends. Shortly after a friend and I fought off an attempted mugging in South Africa and in the last two months my step-father has been in and out of hospital for surgery on his brain.

All of these things have demonstrated to me just how much I am living the philosophies in these pages. Despite my loss and the immense amount of energy and change I have had to go through in a short amount of time, I am grateful for everything that has happened in ways that would otherwise be unimaginable.

My relationship separation gave me the space to step into my power, find my masculine and feminine balance and authentically open myself to a new kind of relationship going forwards.

The sudden loss of my father increased the bond between my sisters and I, at the same time as helping us to see and learn from aspects of ourselves that we previously hadn't encountered. I am so proud of how graceful and gracious we all were throughout.

The attempted mugging was a mirror for the subconscious fear I experienced immediately post separation, what I broadcast out I attracted in and the fact that we managed to fight him off showed me how strong women can be in their masculine when they need to be.

The ongoing situation with my step-father has meant that I have prioritised my time as much as I can to spend with him. I feel that we are closer and have a better understanding of each other because of this and I will never stop appreciating the one gift of time that this has given me with my mum.

Throughout it all, I have not seen any of the situations as bad. By labelling them as bad, I would not be able to learn from them and heal as quickly as I have. I haven't felt blame or anger, just deep love and compassion for everyone involved and affected, enabling me to authentically hold space for us all when I've needed to.

Of course, if I had the choice before these things happened, I wouldn't have consciously chosen them but Shine and our philosophies aren't about that. This mindset is about changing your perception of what happened and using the energy this creates to develop new ways of living and being that ensure that the catalyst for change can eventually lead to something beneficial.

Some of the most amazing and inspirational thought leadership and initiatives have been born out of what most would consider terrible tragedies. Through scarlet fever Helen Keller lost her sight and hearing when she was very young making it virtually impossible to understand what was happening around her and to communicate how she was feeling. It would be easy to pity her descent into silence and darkness but out of this place she learned to speak by tracing words on the palm of her hand and eventually she became a famous advocate for women's suffrage, the poor and the disabled. Something that might not have been possible if she didn't have the illness.

I want to reiterate something I said at the beginning of this book. Every single thing that we create in our lives whether consciously or not, is here to teach us something and if we can open our minds to the learning, our ability to have realisations, heal and process will become that much more effortless.

As you learn and change you will create abundance and as you move away from blame and attachments to labels you will begin to experience unconditional love.

I want to check out of this process with an immense amount of gratitude to each of you that has chosen to take the Shine journey and also with excitement for what I am sure you will go on to create as a result.

Now it is your time to Shine.

Note:

The Shine journey does not have to end with this book. For those that want to take a deeper dive into the philosophies and be taken virtually through a facilitated process we have created the Shine Online Masterclasses. This will connect you with a community of likeminded people, all going through the programme so you can share stories, questions, outputs and ideas with Shine alumni all over the world. For more information visit https:// www.roundtable.global/shine-online.